Elias Canetti's Counter-Image of Society

The award of the Nobel Prize for literature in 1981 has seemingly assured Elias Canetti's place in literary history. But his significance as a cultural critic has not been adequately recognized. The present study redresses this situation in two ways: by mapping the counter-image of human existence, history, and society that informs Canetti's critique of the modern world and its sciences; and by opening up Canetti's hermetic oeuvre by tracing his cryptic and often concealed dialogue with major figures within the Western tradition such as Hobbes, Durkheim, and Freud and contemporaries such as Adorno, Arendt, and Elias. The authors ask how Canetti's alternative vision of man and society relates to important themes of twentieth-century social and civilizational thought even as it calls into question fundamental assumptions of the social and human sciences. In analyses of *Auto da Fé*, *Crowds and Power*, and the aphorisms, the authors elucidate key aspects of Canetti's interrogation of human existence and human history across five thematic complexes: individual and social psychology, totalitarian politics, religion and politics, theories of society, and power and culture. They thus trace the movement of Canetti's thought from an apocalyptic sense of crisis to his search for cultural resources to set against the holocaust of European civilization.

Johann P. Arnason teaches sociology at La Trobe University, Melbourne, and David Roberts is Emeritus Professor of German at Monash University, Melbourne.

Studies in German Literature, Linguistics, and Culture

Edited by James Hardin
(*South Carolina*)

ELIAS CANETTI'S
COUNTER-IMAGE OF SOCIETY
Crowds, Power, Transformation

Johann P. Arnason
and
David Roberts

CAMDEN HOUSE

First published 2004
by Camden House

Camden House is an imprint of Boydell & Brewer Inc.
668 Mt. Hope Avenue, Rochester, NY 14620, USA
www.camden-house.com
and of Boydell & Brewer Limited
PO Box 9, Woodbridge, Suffolk IP12 3DF, UK
www.boydell.co.uk

ISBN: 1-57113-160-4

Library of Congress Cataloging-in-Publication Data

Arnason, Johann Päll, 1940–
    Elias Canetti's counter-image of society: crowds, power, transforma-
tion / Johann P. Arnason and David Roberts
        p. cm. — (Studies in German literature, linguistics, and culture)
    Includes bibliographical references and index.
    ISBN 1-57113-160-4 (alk. paper)
    1. Canetti, Elias, 1905 — Criticism and interpretation.   2. Canetti,
Elias, 1905 — Political and social views.   I. Roberts, David, 1937–
II. Title.   III. Series: Studies in German literature, linguistics, and
culture (Unnumbered)

PT2605.A58Z52 2004
833'.912—dc22
                                                            2003024563

A catalogue record for this title is available from the British Library.

This publication is printed on acid-free paper.
Printed in the United States of America.

For Leslie Bodi

Es gibt kein Ende für den schöpferischen Gedanken des Menschen.
In diesem Fluch liegt die einzige Hoffnung.
Canetti, *Die Provinz des Menschen*

Contents

Abbreviations and Acknowledgments

The following works of Canetti are identified by abbreviations:

AF *Auto da Fé*

AZ *Aufzeichnungen 1992–1993*

CP *Crowds and Power*

GU *Das Geheimherz der Uhr: Aufzeichnungen 1973–1985*

GW *Das Gewissen der Worte: Essays*

NH *Nachträge aus Hampstead: Aus den Aufzeichnungen 1954–1971*

PM *Die Provinz des Menschen: Aufzeichnungen 1942–1972*

Other abbreviations used are:

CM J. S. McClelland, *The Crowd and the Mob from Plato to Canetti*

DE Max Horkheimer and Theodor W. Adorno, *Dialectic of Enlightenment*

DW Marcel Gauchet, *The Disenchantment of the World: A Political History of Religion*

GP "Group Psychology and the Analysis of the Ego" in *The Penguin Freud Library XII*

OT Hannah Arendt, *The Origins of Totalitarianism*, 3rd ed.

Quotations from *Auto da Fé* by Elias Canetti, published by Jonathan Cape, are used by permission of The Random House Group Limited.

Quotations from *Crowds and Power* by Elias Canetti, published by Victor Gollanz, are used by permission of The Orion Publishing Group.

Introduction

D ESPITE THE PUBLICITY associated with the awarding of the Nobel Prize for literature in 1981, Elias Canetti remains an outsider, whose significance as a seminal cultural-diagnostic thinker of our century has not been adequately recognized. His distinctive anti-systematic form of theorizing, which cuts across the customary boundaries between genres and between imagination and theory, confronts the interpreter with particular difficulties. If his place in literary history seems assured, due above all to his one novel *Die Blendung* (written 1930–31, published 1935, English translation *Auto da Fé*, 1947) and his three volumes of autobiography, his place in the history of social and political thought is still undetermined. The distinctive theoretical contribution of *Masse und Macht* (1960, English translation *Crowds and Power*, 1962) presents a challenge that has scarcely been tackled.

Behind the lengthy gestation of *Crowds and Power* lies the deciding experience of the crowd for Canetti in Frankfurt in 1922 (the murder of Rathenau) and in Vienna in 1927 (the burning of the Palace of Justice). His life's work revolves around the task of exploring the significance of the crowd in history against the background and challenge of the crisis of European culture and society and the mass politics of totalitarianism, the central phenomenon of the twentieth century and the test case for all social theory. It is this crisis that he has in mind when he speaks of seizing the century by the throat. His metaphor can, however, also be understood as aiming at the century where it is most vulnerable: in its blind assumptions of progress.

Our book has a double aim. On the one hand we seek to elucidate the counter-image of human being, history, and society that informs Canetti's critique of the modern world and its sciences. On the other we seek to open up his hermetic oeuvre by tracing his cryptic and often concealed dialogue with major figures and tendencies within the Western tradition and by situating him within the intellectual context of his time. Here in particular we ask how his alternative vision of man and society relates to important themes of twentieth-century social and civilizational thought at the same time as it calls into question the assumptions of the social and human sciences.

Our study consists of five interrelated chapters based on *Auto da Fé,* *Crowds and Power,* and the aphorisms. The intention of the analyses is exemplary rather than exhaustive, directed to illuminating key aspects of Canetti's interrogation of human being and human history across five thematic complexes: individual and social psychology, totalitarian politics, religion and politics, and theories of society, power, and culture. At the same time the order of the chapters is designed to trace the movement of Canetti's thought from an apocalyptic sense of crisis to his search for cultural resources to set against the blindness of his times.

The setting of *Auto da Fé* is Vienna, the breeding ground since the turn of the century of the new mass politics which emerged out of the crisis of nineteenth-century liberalism and the First World War. Canetti radicalizes the cultural critique of the epoch — the vitalist denunciations of sterile intellectualism and crippled life — in terms of the crowd, the "mass-soul" within each of us, threatening the apocalypse of the atomistic "society of individuals" (chapter 1). The scope and meaning of his master concept of the crowd and of the mass-soul as they are developed in the novel are examined with reference to the individual and social psychology of Sigmund Freud, Norbert Elias, and Cornelius Castoriadis.

If *Auto da Fé* was the prophetic anticipation of the holocaust of civilization, *Crowds and Power* is the attempt after the catastrophe to provide a genealogy of totalitarianism (chapter 2). Canetti's sharp distinction between crowds and power is seen as crucial to his rejection of the late nineteenth-century psychology and pathology of the crowd, which culminates in Freud's theories, and to an understanding of what separates him from the theoretical accounts of totalitarianism in the writings of his contemporaries and fellow refugees from National Socialism, Theodor Adorno, Max Horkheimer, and Hannah Arendt.

Canetti's "natural history" of modernity, central to his genealogy of totalitarianism, involves a reversal of our familiar evolutionary versions of history, thereby challenging the most basic assumptions of modern historical consciousness. The critical significance of Canetti's anti-evolutionism appears particularly clearly in the reconstruction of the religious history of politics embedded in *Crowds and Power,* which we examine and evaluate through a close comparison with the political history of religion proposed by Marcel Gauchet in *The Disenchantment of the World* (chapter 3).

Canetti's image of man and society is best understood as a radical challenge to dominant modes of social thought, both those of the mainstream sociological tradition and the less successful countercurrent of mass psychology from Le Bon to Freud (chapter 4). Notwithstanding the absence of direct references, Canetti's theoretical work relates to these unequally developed approaches in critical as well as constructive ways. His objections to over-integrated and over-rationalized models of society have some points of contact with mass psychology, but his distinctive interpretation of crowd experiences sets him apart from all precursors. The new understanding of crowds and their instituting potential opens up new perspectives on the whole social-historical field, not least in regard to power and its changing forms.

Canetti's concept of transformation was, as he saw it, a master key to the mutations of power and their cultural sources. But it also signals a new grasp of the human capacities and characteristics that resist complete absorption or utilization by power (chapter 5). The transformational aspect of human nature, variously highlighted in Canetti's aphorisms, is more elusive than the mainsprings of power; only a combination of both themes will add up to a balanced counter-image of society. More specifically, the concept of trans-formation can be understood — despite Canetti's aversion to the conven-tional language of cultural theory — as an attempt to rethink the cultural dimension of the "human province."

Canetti's "human province" is still for the most part the province of liter-ary scholarship. In the case of the novel and the aphorisms we can speak of a productive reception. Since its re-publication in the 1960s *Auto da Fé* has been the object of ongoing interest, evident in a steady stream of monographs and articles.[1] Although the aphorisms have received less attention, a number of studies have begun to map the rich corpus of reflections that document Canetti's thinking across some fifty years.[2] *Crowds and Power*, the central but uncompleted work of maturity, presents a different picture. On the one hand it has been ignored by the social sciences,[3] on the other it has proved resistant to the approaches of literary scholars. The attempts to remedy this impasse through cross-disciplinary colloquia have been less than successful. Colloquia of this kind seldom achieve interdisciplinary synergies. The conference volumes devoted to *Crowds and Power*,[4] however welcome, cannot take the place of a systematic investigation of Canetti's magnum opus.

Although *Crowds and Power* figures prominently in the following chapters we have no such ambition. Our aim is rather to complement the existing literature on Canetti with its primary orientation to the disciplinary interests and perspectives of literary studies. For our purposes, it is more important to bring Canetti's work into contact with broader contexts and currents of social theory, than to situate our interpretation within a *Rezeptionsgeschichte* that has mostly taken a different direction. References to the growing literature on

Canetti are therefore kept to a necessary and selective minimum in favor of a discussion of elective affinities and of possible combinations with ideas from other sources. This approach may seem alien to Canetti's own intentions: as he put it, he feared the "Aristotelianization" of his thoughts, and there is no doubt about his hostility to every kind of systematic theory.[5] In that sense, we must invoke the time-honored hermeneutical claim to understand an author better than he understood himself. It would not be unfair to describe our project as an exercise in limited and controlled Aristotelianization. We are, in other words, convinced that latent meanings of Canetti's work call for more explicit conceptual articulation and more sustained confrontation with other attempts to make sense of the same historical experiences. But this is not to deny the radically unorthodox and anti-systematic character of Canetti's theorizing. We have tried to strike the right balance between constructive interpretation and sensitivity to the unique features of an outsider's project. The five chapters, the first three by David Roberts, the last two by Johann P. Arnason, are thus perhaps best read as interconnected explorations of a thematic complex — the relations between culture and power — that by its very nature does not lend itself to exhaustive treatment.

1: The Auto-da-Fé of Civilization

IN THE SECOND VOLUME of his autobiography Canetti recalls the burning of the Palace of Justice in Vienna in 1927. The events of that day of riots and violence were to be seminal: from the experience of the mysterious and contagious power of the crowd came the central theme of his life's work, and an image — an official of the Ministry of Justice surrounded by burning files — which was to act as a catalyst for *Auto da Fé*, written three years later.[1] The novel unfolds an apocalyptic vision of European society on the edge of the volcano, blind to its destructive other, the eruptive force of the crowd. What Canetti understands by the crowd is the focus of the present chapter, since it forms the imaginative background to his subsequent writings without ever appearing again in such a comprehensive, mythical fashion. I say "mythical" in order to characterize Canetti's antithetical stance towards the scientific appropriation of the world, which must be seen in the context of the cultural criticism of the time (Cultural Crisis). To the onto-logic of the "head" the novel opposes a mytho-logic of the "world," which is explored in relation to the blindness of philosophy to the Heraclitean flux of being, the "magma" underlying the western tradition of ontology (The World as Magma and Monad), in relation to the blindness of sociology to the other of the "society of individuals" and its negative anthropology (The Society of Individuals), and in relation to the blindness of psychology to the "mass-soul" beneath our supposed individuality (The Mass-Soul). The last section returns to the theme of cultural critique, the tension between life and forms, in order to open up the concept of transformation in the novel in the light of mythical thought (Life, Form, Transformation).

Cultural Crisis

Canetti's original title for his one novel — "Kant catches fire" — provides the link between the German title — "Die Blendung" (blindness, the blinding) — and the authorized English title, "Auto da Fé": the blindness of philosophy leads to its self-immolation. The novel ends with the scholar Peter Kien setting fire to his library. The burning of the books can be seen as embracing not only the end of this novel but the apocalypse of the novel form as such, the genre of the bourgeois epoch and the bourgeois individual, the genre defined by the separation of "soul" and "world" (Lukács), "head" and "world" (Canetti).[2] In his *Theory of the Novel* (1920), Lukács envisaged a new community and a new epic beyond the negativities of bourgeois society and the bourgeois novel. The generic blindness of philosophy and of the novel thus converge in *Auto da Fé* in a suicidal self-critique, which likewise points beyond itself to the other side of the novel's fatal progression from "head without world" (Part I) via "headless world" (Part II) to the madness of "world in the head" (Part III). This otherness is indicated (negatively) by the *anti-concept* of the crowd (die Masse, translated as "mass" in the novel), which stands for *anti-thesis* as such: the negation of all conceptual delimitations, determinations and distinctions: in other words, the indeterminate to which conceptual thought is by definition blind. As the negation of the principle of individuation, the idea and the experience of the "crowd" cancels the common-sense separation of head and world and its philosophical underpinnings — the Cartesian split between subject and object, Kant's distinction between phenomenon and noumenon. The Kantian legacy of the thing-in-itself returns, however, in Schopenhauer and Nietzsche's metaphysics of the Will, stages in the conflagration of philosophy, whose drastic conclusion is signaled by *Auto da Fé*.

"Kant catches fire" accordingly signifies the process of the self-destruction of the Cartesian construction of the world and of the philosophy of consciousness. In this trial of monadic consciousness Canetti's novel resumes and radicalizes the whole thrust of *Lebensphilosophie*, a term which came to the fore in the 1920s although it goes back to Schopenhauer's opposing of "life," of the Will, to the principles of German idealism. Herbert Schnädelbach sees in this vitalistic attack on the whole tradition of western rationalism, combined with cultural pessimism and a tragic sense of life, the sum of the epoch 1880–1930.[3] From Nietzsche to Bergson and Klages the opposition of "life" and "spirit" became the leitmotif and dominating theme of an omnipresent cultural critique. The Nietzschean "optic of life" raised the intuitive opposition between the living and the dead, the healthy and the sick, the creative and the sterile to the normative criterion of a metaphysics of irrationalism, which viewed reason and rationality as epiphenomena of the life force. Once the intellect turns against life man becomes crippled (Nietzsche), the neurotic product of modern civilization (Freud); once man's objectivations become alien to him we have the "tragedy of culture" (Simmel); once the past gains ascendancy over the present then knowledge, separating itself from life, becomes deadly. In short, the petrified world of a frozen second nature, the object of analysis by Simmel, Lukács, and Benjamin, confronts modern man with a fatal but also fatally ambivalent dialectic of civilization: if "spirit" is the enemy of "soul" (Klages), if consciousness is a deadly curse, does the longed-for breakthrough to "life" herald the rejuvenating liberation from alienation or the destruction of all forms of mediation?[4]

This ambivalence has been written into the "progress" of philosophy since Kant. The reduction of reason to history and in turn of history to life finds its counterpoint in a cultural critique which appeals to the spontaneity of unconscious forces, to the primacy of the *élan vital* over the reifications of rationalism. *Auto da Fé* can thus draw on a whole arsenal of vitalist *topoi*, based on the opposition between the living and the dead (body/mind, unconscious/conscious, flux/form, spontaneity/rigidity, etc.) — an opposition that is *embodied* and personified in the brothers Peter and George Kien: Peter, the foremost Sinologist of the age, who has devoted himself to the solitary life of the mind in his windowless library in Vienna, George, psychiatrist and director of a mental asylum in Paris, who has turned his back on the fashionable vogue for psychoanalysis in order to immerse himself in the electric atmosphere of his mad patients. George appears as *deus ex machina* in the third part of the novel, summoned to the rescue of his brother from the clutches of his housekeeper wife, Therese, in alliance with the brutal caretaker, Benedikt Pfaff. Peter's blindness to his nemesis, Therese (whose name Krummholz, "crooked timber," denotes the intractable otherness of "life" to Kantian reason), leads to his expulsion from his library, dispossession and incarceration. George functions at the same time as the prophet of the breakthrough to true reality, inspired by his patients to dispel the blindness of the "head," of science, to the "crowd" within the individual. He is convinced that the unconscious power of the "mass-soul" provides the key not only to the obsessions and delusions of his patients but to the psyche in general.

With the introduction of the (anti-)concept of the crowd, Canetti gives a crucial twist to the critique of bourgeois society: George draws on another — parallel and reverse — line of civilizational theory, the nineteenth-century discourse of the crowd, regarded as constituting the ever-present threat of the eruption of atavistic natural forces destructive of the whole process of civilization.[5] In relation to the (discourse of the) crowd, which marks the sociopolitical interface between civilizational theory and the political history of bourgeois society since the French Revolution, the blindness of cultural critique appears particularly clearly in its schizophrenic ambivalence towards the "return of the repressed," which combined fear and contempt for the cultureless masses with calls to live dangerously and adulation of the blond beast. The negative "process of civilization," as construed by Nietzsche and Freud, can be viewed as the complement to the crowd discourse of the epoch, just as conversely Georges Sorel's *Reflexions on Violence* stands at the opposite pole to Norbert Elias's reconstruction of the history of the "pacification of the human soul" in *The Civilizing Process*, written in the shadow of the Third Reich.[6] If fin-de-siècle France was the place of the birth of crowd psychology and of fascist ideology, fin-de-siècle Vienna was the site of the new politics based on the mobilization of the urban masses.[7] Hitler, the assiduous reader of Le Bon's *Psychology of the Crowd*, and Mussolini, the great admirer of Sorel, spearheaded the transformation of the cultural critique of decadent civilization, this "revolt of the feelings und instincts, of energy, of the will, and of primal forces" into political revolution against liberal democracy and the bourgeois "system."[8] The apocalyptic finale of Canetti's novel appears as a direct anticipation of the book burnings of 1933. Whatever else, the end of the novel signals the limits of fiction in relation to the world and its political convulsions.[9]

On the other side of the novel lie the Third Reich and Canetti's turn from fiction to the systematic study of crowds and power. It is therefore important to stress the negativity, indicated by the novel's title, which embraces all the figures. The brothers Peter and George articulate from opposite sides the dialectic of civilization. They function as opposed embodiments of the fundamental ambivalence of bourgeois society to its destructive-redemptive other. Peter Kien's name alludes to the transformation of the lifeless into the living, of stone into fire (Kienspan — kindling wood). It is Peter, the man of character, who surrenders to the crowd, not George, the actor, who like all the advocates of apocalyptic politics cannot resist playing with fire. His blindness to the plight of his brother, his haste to return to the mental asylum, where he is just as much the absolute ruler as his brother is in his windowless library, underlines the novel's bleak monadism: the vision of society as a universe of self-centered atoms. Moreover, the novel of blindness implies, as mentioned, the blindness of the novel form as the medium of bourgeois individuality and subjectivity. Canetti replaces the paradigmatic narrative of the bourgeois subject — the *Bildungsroman* — with its negation — the novel of blindness. The critique of "Bildung," defined and dismissed by George as a *cordon sanitaire* against the reality and the experience of the crowd, goes together with references to "Rückbildung" (involution): the novel of development reverses into the involution of the process of civilization, graphically exemplified by the patient who cures George of his educated misconceptions, a madman who has transformed himself into a gorilla (an episode conceived expressly in counterpoint to Kafka's *Metamorphosis* and its version of the crippling effects of civilization). The critique of the blindness of "Bildung" may indeed gesture towards the *Aufhebung* (sublation) of the bourgeois subject and the bourgeois novel in the flames which consume Peter Kien and his books, but the novel itself is inescapably characterized by its ironic negativities, which undercut the positions of all the figures. Precisely this tragic-comic play of blind positions distinguishes *Auto da Fé*, if not from a comparable sense of crisis, at least from the fatal simplifications of the cultural critique of the 1920s.

The World as Magma and Monad

We could render Canetti's distinction between Head and World not only in terms of Lukács's Soul and World but also of Schopenhauer's division of the world into Will and Representation, a division which is of its very nature blind in that it masks the underlying monism of the World as Will. The World as Magma and Monad likewise links blindness and perception. "Monad" takes up the unmistakable reference to Leibniz's *Monadology* in the novel. If Peter Kien in his windowless library epitomizes the blindness of the head, he is only the most extreme image of the monadic isolation that has produced the "society of individuals." "Magma" is Cornelius Castoriadis's term for the mode of being of everything that is prior to its conceptual determination. It is particularly apposite in relation to the Heraclitean ontology, which informs Canetti's mythical sense of the world. The mythical and the magmatic belong together since both call into question the identity-thinking of Western metaphysics. As the indeterminate, magma designates the initial stratum of the "world," which cannot be exhausted by the onto-logic of the "head," determined to absorb within itself even its "chaotic" antithesis. Moreover, it is precisely the onto-logical division between the determinate and the indeterminate which is undercut by the magmatic being of things. Referring to the *locus classicus* of the distinction between the limit and the unlimited in Plato's *Philebus*, Castoriadis speaks of "the holding-together of distinct-indistinct components of a manifold,"[10] involving a hybrid relation between the definite and the indefinite, which confounds the philosopher's task of giving measure to the measureless (Plato). This hybrid relation means that the traditional ontology of the thing as substance-essence (or of the monadic subject), complete and closed on itself, is no more than an illusory representation, just as denotation on closer scrutiny dissolves into a magma of connotations: if the name Socrates does not normally imply "somato-psychical Heraclitean flux, dance of electrons and of representations,"[11] it is because the head is blind to the magmatic continuum of which it is part.

Peter Kien is led to question this blindness. Defenseless against Therese's invasion of his library space (the housekeeper employed for years to protect his books from the accumulation of dust, whose service he rewards in a fatally weak moment by marriage), he resolves to shut his eyes, literally not metaphorically, to the "dazzling furniture" disturbing his concentration. The new weapon of blindness produces of itself the "necessary philosophy."

> Blindness is a weapon against time and space; our being is one vast blindness, save only for that little circle which our mean intelligence — mean in its nature as in its scope — can illumine. The dominating principle of the universe is blindness. . . . Shapes to which one man as well as another may well be blind, fill Kien's room, his fingers, his books. This printed page, clear and coordinated as any other, is in reality an inferno of furious electrons. If he were perpetually conscious of this, the letters would dance before his eyes. His fingers would feel the pressure of their evil motion like so many needle pricks. In a single day he might manage to achieve one feeble line, no more. It is his right to apply that blindness, which protects him from the excesses of the senses, to every disturbing element in his life. (*AF*, 79)

We can set against Peter's rationalization of the blindness "by which the seeing live" his subsequent dream of a volcano about to erupt. Peter, the man of stone, who transforms himself into an Egyptian statue in a last desperate defense against Therese (the chapter "Petrification"), will finally become molten rock. The commentary to his dream is given in his reflections, provoked by Therese's occupation of three of the four rooms of the apartment, which has led to his physical separation from his "library-body." The complement to his philosophy of blindness, designed to protect him from the excesses of the senses, is his awakened sensibility to the ambivalence of the expression "dead matter."

> Many times he reproached himself for thus of his own free will mutilating a living organism, his own creation. Books have no life; they lack feeling maybe, and perhaps cannot feel pain, as animals and even plants feel pain. But what proof have we that inorganic objects can feel no

pain? Who knows if a book may not yearn for other books, its com-
panion of many years, in some way strange to us and therefore never
yet perceived? Every thinking being knows those moments in which the
traditional frontier set by science between the organic and the inorganic
seems artificial and outdated, like every frontier drawn by men. Is not
a secret antagonism to this division revealed in the very phrase "dead
matter"? For the dead must once have been the living. Let us admit
then of a substance that it is *dead*, have we not in so doing endowed it
with an erstwhile *life*? (*AF*, 75)

Peter's reflections have both a critical and a mythical point. The knowledge that the dead must once have been the living adds to the scientific
division between the organic and the inorganic the historical division between the past and the present. It tells us that the animating force of *Wissenschaft* springs from the (necrophiliac) attraction to the erstwhile life of
ancient texts and dead languages (just as the thought of Therese's death
instantly kindles Peter's love). Peter's library is an Egyptian kingdom of the
dead, from which life has been excluded: "He longed for the future, because
then there would be more past in the world" (*AF*, 177). His "historical
method" — "to master a fellow-creature, it suffices to find his place in
history" — fails utterly, however, before the analphabetic Therese, whose
only thought is of money and sex: "As far as he was familiar with the history
of all cultures and barbarisms there was not one into which Therese would
have fitted" (*AF*, 128). The barbarian at the gates is an ancient and recurrent
refrain of civilization. It enables Peter to "place" the doorkeeper Pfaff: he is
the *Landsknecht*, the enlisted barbarian mercenary, born into the wrong
century. Therese, however, is life itself, which Peter has mindlessly allowed
entrance by surrendering the keys to his library-heaven. That the Chinese
Wall protecting civilization from the barbarians cannot be maintained, that
the enemy without is the enemy within: this is the secret truth behind his
dawning sense of the ambivalence of "dead matter." Or, as Therese indig-
nantly puts it, after beating her impotent husband insensible: "What next,
being alive, when you're dead, whatever next?" (*AF*, 120)

In the "dead matter" that is waiting to return to life, in the living that
is treated as "dead matter," Canetti has transformed the master trope of
Lebensphilosophie, but also equally of Western Marxism (the distinction
between living and dead labor), into an explosive dialectic of reification and
animation. Or rather, bearing the erstwhile title of the novel in mind, we
should say that his aim, impelled by the magmatic being of things, is to set
these concepts on fire, on the one hand by revealing the magmatic being of

language, and on the other by breaking down the boundaries between the theoretical and the mythical, thereby invalidating in equally destructive fashion the "rational" distinction between the rational and the irrational, enlightenment and myth, and the intuitive, "irrational" distinction between soul and spirit, life and forms. Schelling's characterization of language as a faded mythology points to the dialectic of living and dead metaphor in the novel, which bears witness to the "life" inhabiting concepts and to the violence at work in both maintaining and dissolving conceptual boundaries. To give but one example of the "mytho-logical" fusion of the reification and animation at work everywhere in the novel: Peter has dedicated his life to turning the family capital into books, Therese once she has gained possession of the library sets out to reverse the process. She spends her time counting the books and adding up the totals, aided by the magic operator "0," which multiplies the result millionfold. In "0," the "leaping" and the "annihilating" number, Canetti captures the imaginary power of the identical *par excellence*: numbers and money, summed up in the fearful dialectic of growth and depreciation, analyzed in *Crowds and Power* in relation to the effects of inflation in the Weimar Republic. The National Socialists were able to turn the dynamic of this "witches' Sabbath of devaluation" against the Jews, repeating the process of mass devaluation and mass annihilation.[12]

The field force of the crowd (in all its aspects) negates the neat polarities of cultural critique and nullifies the dreams of a synthesis between head and world. The tripartite structure of the novel replicates the familiar pattern of diremption and redemptive reunion the better to demonstrate the self-destructive consequences of reunion. "World in the Head" savagely parodies the vanishing point of cultural critique: the *coincidentia oppositorum*, the aesthetic fusion of form and living content, which inspired contemporary redemptive visions as diverse as Lukács's projection of the proletariat as the identical subject-object of history or Hofmannsthal's dream of a synthesis of life and spirit in a "conservative revolution." If with Canetti we reverse perspectives, we can see that the blindness, "by which the seeing live," is the condition of the onto-logic and the onto-dialectic of Western philosophy. If Lukács, or Horkheimer and Adorno in *Dialectic of Enlightenment*, argue that bourgeois thought is condemned to regress to myth, and that mythology, in Lukács's words, "inevitably adopts the structure of the problem whose opacity has been the cause of its own birth,"[13] then *Auto da Fé* lays bare this catastrophic structure of opacity.

The Society of Individuals

In 1939, following completion of his magnum opus, *The Civilizing Process*, Norbert Elias devoted a short study to exposing and dissolving the paradox of the "society of individuals," which posed the conundrum of the link between these two "self-evidently" distinct entities: "individual" and "society."[14] For Canetti it was precisely this conundrum of unconnected co-existence that defined the crisis of contemporary society and provided the impetus to writing the novel: "One day it struck me that . . . the world had fallen apart, and only if you had the courage to show it in its disintegration was it still possible to give a truthful representation of it."[15] Canetti's dissolution of the "blind" antithesis between the individual and society is diametrically opposed to that of Elias. Their theme, however, is the same: the process of civilization which has led to the gulf between head and world, to the alienation diagnosed in Freud's *Civilization and its Discontents*[16] or in Klages's *Der Geist als Widersacher der Seele* (Mind as Antagonist of the Soul), cultural diagnoses exactly contemporary with the writing of *Auto da Fé*. Behind Freud, Klages, Canetti, and Elias (and likewise Horkheimer and Adorno's *Dialectic of Enlightenment*) stands the figure of Nietzsche and a host of Nietzschean "prophets of despair," caught in a blind ambivalence towards the taming of the drives and the consequent pacification of "life." *The Civilizing Process* continues and corrects Nietzsche's *Genealogy of Morals* in its reconstruction of the transformation of the "blond beast" into the polished courtier of the seventeenth century. What Elias calls the "courtization of the warriors" provides the precondition and prototype of the subsequent progressive internalization of social controls under the pressure of fear and anxiety, the pressure, that is, of a strong super-ego, leading to the highly regulated behavior of contemporary society. Elias's psycho/sociogenesis of the modern individual describes Canetti's "head without world." It has nothing to say, however, about Canetti's "headless world" of the lumpenproletariat, the pimps, prostitutes, and petty criminals of the urban underworld, or about the madness of the "world in the head" that conjures up the suicidal apocalypse of the "society of individuals." It is thus not by chance that George Kien regards novels as the successors to the books of manners and their civilizing function, analyzed by Elias. George dismisses all fiction as a "textbook of manners" (*AF*, 447). Ensconced in the haven of the Reading Room of the British Library from the time of his arrival as a refugee in Great Britain in 1934, Elias seems as blind as Peter Kien in his library to events outside. It is distressing to register that the second edition of his book is dedicated to his mother, murdered in Auschwitz five years after the publication of the first edition in 1939, and that the Introduction added to the second German edition (which is not included in the English translation) has not a word to say about the "civilizational rupture" of the Holocaust.

Nevertheless, the central theme of this Introduction (which draws closely on the 1939 study on the society of individuals) is blindness, the blindness of modern Western *homo clausus*, whose self-understanding is both product and corollary of the civilizing process, which has set up invisible walls separating "head" and "world," "subject" and "object," "ego" and "others," "individual" and "society." Like Canetti, Elias regards *egocentrism* as the source of our blindness, and like Canetti, he observes its ramifications everywhere. The Introduction can thus serve as an introduction to the "blindness" of the "civilizing process" as theorized by Elias and exemplified by Canetti. What both demonstrate is a *reification of perception* in relation to the world, to society, to the self and others. Indeed, the blindness of *Wissenschaft* to life, to the "living person as a whole" (Elias),[17] forms the ground bass, as we have seen, of the epoch. Elias and Canetti share with *Lebensphilosophie* and Heideggerian phenomenology the revolt against the "head without world," the ego-logical subject of knowledge.

Elias links the modern, scientific relation to "external" nature to the new personality structures based on the control of the emotions. The level of self-distancing and "objectivity" thereby attained transforms nature into a lifeless material complex, subject to laws and devoid of purpose, which has meaning for us only in terms of our ability to control and manipulate it. The exclusion of the person of the scientist, that is, of the self-controlled subject as the condition of science, from the field of investigation means that the whole process of self-distancing appears as a self-evident spatial separation of "inner" subject and "external" object. Conversely, the blocking of affective impulses towards the objects of thought manifests itself in the sense of enclosure in a "cage," which blocks the access of the "self," of "existence," of "reason" to the world "outside." The inhibition of physical contact accordingly privileges the eye as the pure, transparent instrument of cognition. As Elias puts it, the epistemological subject gains knowledge of the world and its objects simply by opening his eyes: *esse percipi* concludes Peter Kien. That the theoretical gaze is blind to its own blindness is the common theme of Elias and Canetti: both emphasize the blocking of affect, which reduces dynamic processes to inert states, the energetic flux of relations to dead matter.

For Elias this process of the disenchantment of the world and the disembodiment of the (cognitive) subject is enshrined in philosophy since

Descartes and in contemporary sociology: *homo sociologicus* presupposes *homo philosophicus,* the philosophical ideal of the free, autonomous personality, independent of others. The "self in its shell" forms one of the constant topoi of modern philosophy from the thinking ego of Descartes, the windowless monads of Leibniz, and the Kantian subject of cognition, to the solitary individuals of existential philosophy. This separation of individual and society returns in sociology in Weber's distinction between the "social" and the "non-social" actions of individuals or in Parsons' separation of "ego" and "system." Elias takes functional sociology to task for its concepts, such as "structure," "function," "norm," "integration," which are abstracted from the developmental character of the social process. At issue for Elias is the question: can the egocentric image of society as an aggregation of separate and independent individuals, each a world for itself, can the epistemological division of the social universe into inner and outer worlds, provide an adequate basis for social theory? For Canetti it is the question whether such a "society of individuals," encapsulated in themselves and incapable of communication, can survive. For both, the crucial issue involves a rethinking of the relationship between the "individual" and "society" and its corollaries, a rethinking of the relationship of the individual to the self and others and to "internal" and "external" nature. It calls, says Elias, for a *Copernican revolution,* which replaces *homo clausus* by the priority of the social group, that is, the replacement of the closed personality by the image of the open personality, oriented to others and dependent upon them (lxvii). In the brothers Peter and George, Canetti presents the paradigmatic opposition between the closed and the open personality. It is in fact an ironic contrast, since it is marked by blindness on both sides. Canetti also sets out in his novel to effect a Copernican revolution, aimed at dislodging the ego-centered individual from the center of the social universe, but where Elias proposes the social group as the mediating figuration between the false alternatives of individual and society, Canetti presents the reversal of the supposed individual into the crowd. And where Elias takes the *dance* as his image for the plurality of mutually oriented inter-dependent individuals (lxviii), Canetti makes it the mythic image of the joyous release from the burden of individuation in the crowd:

> Therese dances up and down, her skirt sways. A powerful rhythm seizes on the crowd. Some sway this way, some that, the zest of the movement increases . . . The Theresianium, always alive with action, is filled with a gigantic calm. One panting breath alone reveals that it still lives.

All living creatures in its huge population draw in one single deep breath together, and together, ecstatic, breathe it out again. (*AF,* 330)

Compared with Canetti, Elias, we may say, registers only the one side of the dialectic of the civilizing process. His subject is the *civilized,* that is to say, the *socialized* human being, whether we refer to the closed personality as the product of the civilizing process or to his counter-image of the open personality. Elias stresses the civilizing force of the super-ego, not the revolt of the id. This means on the one hand that he sees the "cripples" but not the "beasts," and on the other that his view of social man does not reckon with what in man resists the intertwined process of socialization and individuation, that is, what Canetti in the novel calls the "mass-soul." Here we may note that *Crowds and Power* begins with liberation from the fear, dictated by self-preservation, which draws the boundaries of the personality and constitutes the individual, and that *Auto da Fé* ends with the laughter of Peter Kien as he is engulfed by the flames of his library.

The negative dialectic of the individual and the crowd exemplifies the alternating current of the social field, but not the alternative to the society of individuals. Its corollary is the negative dialectic of cripples and beasts that defines the negative anthropology of the novel. This negative and one-sided dialectic — negative in that the cripples are crippled beasts, one-sided in that the cripples are the victims of the beasts — finds its "sublation" in the crowd, in which cripples become beasts by discharging their crippled being onto a scapegoat: "Cripples ought to be exterminated. All criminals are cripples. No, all cripples are criminals." (*AF,* 367) Peter and George confirm this negative anthropology in their respective versions of self-recognition and blindness. Peter — tall, skeletal, fleshless — is drawn to Fischerle, the hunchbacked dwarf (Don Quixote and Sancho Panza in the city) by the recognition of his "humanity." The scene, set in a church, comes from the chapter entitled appropriately "Revelations":

> "You are hardly human," he [Peter] breathed, lovingly.
> "A deformity is hardly human, is that my fault?"
> "Man is the only deformity," Kien tried his voice a tone stronger.
> He and the dwarf were looking into each other's eyes, so he forgot there were things he shouldn't have mentioned in the dwarf's presence.
> "No," said Fischerle, "man isn't a deformity, or I'd be a man!"
> "No, I won't have that. Man is the only beast!" (*AF,* 275)

Peter's recognition of his own likeness, of his "hardly human" image of man in Fischerle, is matched by George's life-transforming encounter with a "gorilla in human clothes," a "harmless madman," held under lock and key at the house of his brother, a banker:

> From a few powerful words, hurled into the room like living tree trunks, George guessed at some mythical tale of passion, which shattered him with fearful doubts of himself. He saw himself as an insect in the presence of a man. . . . How could he measure himself, sitting at the same table with a creature such as this, he a creature of custom, of favours, with every pore of his soul stuffed with fat, every day more fat, a half-man in all practical uses, without the courage to be. . . . (*AF*, 451)

The "gorilla in human clothes" appears as a *reprise* and reversal of Kafka's *Metamorphosis*: not only does the gorilla triumphantly affirm his involution (Rückbildung), but his impact on George is overwhelming: "He saw himself as an insect in the presence of a man." Turning his back, like Prince Gautama, on the "beautiful" world of professional success and adoring women, George finds the way to the wilderness, where he becomes the "selfless" admirer of his mad patients. And, like Buddha, he discovers in the wilderness the key to the madness and suffering of civilized man: it is our blindness to the unbearable tension between the principle of individuation and the mass-soul. The parallels to Hesse's celebration of vitalism in his most famous novel *Steppenwolf* (1927) should not be overlooked. Like George, whose "one desire was perpetually to lose himself" (462), Hesse's Wolf Man denounces the cowardice of bourgeois man and preaches the Dionysian abandonment of the self:

> Never will he [the bourgeois] surrender himself, abandon himself to intoxication or asceticism, never will he be a martyr, never will he agree to his annihilation — on the contrary, his ideal is not surrender but preservation of the ego. . . . A man cannot live intensely except at the cost of the Self.[18]

The Mass-Soul

Just as the individual is divided between social psychology (Elias) and mass psychology (Le Bon) and the psyche between the opposing forces of the super-ego and the id, so sociology finds itself poised precariously between the discourse of the civilizing process and the discourse of mass society, between theories of the elite (Pareto, Michels) and theories of the masses (Taine, Le

Bon, Sorel).[19] If mass theory emphasizes the threat to civilization represented by the crowd, the theories of mass society since Tocqueville register the correlation between individualization and mass society, the individualization demanded by the transition from *Gemeinschaft* to *Gesellschaft*. Emancipation from the premodern web of associations through the workings of the market, competition, and contract leaves the individual isolated and alienated and poses the question of the viability of the society of individuals. Can society cohere solely on the basis of private interests? Behind this question we can observe a basic anthropological skepticism in relation to the modern individual. Theories of the crowd and of mass society thus necessarily raise the question of the anthropological foundation of the social bond and the civilizing process.[20] The fear of the reversion of culture to nature accompanies the diagnoses of the disintegration and atomization of class society, of the ego weakness of the subject (Adorno), or of the "decisive weakening of the instinct of self-preservation" (Arendt), advanced as causes paving the way for the triumph of totalitarian movements (see chapter 2).

All the threads of the novel's negative anthropology come together in George's theory of the mass-soul, which is directed against the advocates of the "fashionable mania of the time, which filled every head and explained little": Freud's pleasure principle.[21] Although Canetti in the second volume of his autobiography singles out "Group Psychology and Ego Analysis" as the text which sparked his rejection of the psychoanalytic interpretation of the crowd (see chapter 2), it is clear that George's postulation of a mass-soul is to be understood as an answer to Freud's postulation of a death instinct in "Beyond the Pleasure Principle." To Freud's biological speculations on the longing of living beings to return to the inanimate state, George opposes the historical significance of the biological longing of human beings to return to the mass.

> Of that far deeper and most special motive force of history, the desire of men to rise into a higher type of animal, the mass, and to lose themselves in it so completely as to forget that one man ever existed, they had no idea. For they were educated men, and education is in itself a *cordon sanitaire* for the individual against the mass in his own soul.
>
> We wage the so-called war of existence for the destruction of the mass-soul in ourselves, no less than for hunger and love. In certain circumstance it can become so strong as to force the individual to selfless acts or even to acts contrary to their own interests. "Mankind" has existed as a mass for long before it was conceived of and watered down into an idea. It foams, a huge, wild, full-blooded, warm animal in all of us, very deep, far deeper than the maternal. In spite of its age it is the

youngest of the beasts, the essential creation of the earth, its goal and its future. We know nothing of it; we still live, supposedly as individuals. Sometimes the masses pour over us, one single flood, one ocean, in which each drop is alive, and each drop wants the same thing. But it soon scatters again, and leaves us once more to ourselves, poor solitary devils. (*AF*, 461)

The emphasis on the struggle "for the destruction of the mass-soul in ourselves" adds another dimension to the violence of the civilizing process: all the novel's figures are consumed by fantasies of crowds and power, just as countless people, according to George, are driven mad by the crowd in the head that can find no satisfaction. Again we can turn to Castoriadis to elucidate the concept of the mass-soul. Canetti and Castoriadis both locate the division between the individual and society in the individual himself. What Castoriadis calls the monadic core of the psyche, as opposed to the social subject, marks the interface between body and mind, drives and their representation. The monadic core carries a memory, a trace of the original state of the psyche, which reveals itself in daydreams and fantasies:

> The social individual is constructed as divided between the monadic pole, which always tends to lock everything up and to short-circuit it in order to carry it back to an impossible monadic state and failing to do so, to its substitutes, hallucinatory satisfaction and phantasizing . . . [22]

Behind the secondary elaboration of fantasies lies the primordial fantasy of a state of "totalitarian inclusion," in which the self is everything, prior to the distinction between inside and outside. The socialization of the subject thus demands the fracturing of this primary closure, the imposition of the separation and of the otherness of the object, but at the price of an irreducible psychic autism: the phantasm of the "restoration of the initial unity of the subject." It is this desire, master of all desires, of total unification, of the abolition of difference and of distance, manifested above all as being unaware of difference and distance, which, in the field of the unconscious, arranges all the representations that emerge in the direction of its own lines of force.

How is this primal desire, this unconscious drive to be characterized? George speaks of a "huge, wild, full-blooded, warm animal in all of us, very deep, far deeper than the maternal." Castoriadis speaks of the "monster of unifying madness," which reigns as lord and master in the darkest cavern of the unconscious. The two inseparable dimensions of this primal desire — "the tendency towards unification" and "the magical omnipotence of thought"[23] — appear as the dynamic fusion of crowds and power in the fantasies of Canetti's figures: the explosive growth of the crowd feeds the theatre of the megalomaniac self. The "blind" beggar envisions himself in his harem surrounded by hundreds of women, each larger than the next. Fischerle imagines himself as world chess champion and millionaire.[24] In his gigantic palace he plays "in thirty vast halls . . . night and day thirty simultaneous games of chess with living pieces which he has only to command" (*AF*, 226). Peter dreams of doubling his library, Therese of Peter's supposed millions. Even George entertains the fantasy of becoming "People's Commissar for Lunatics": "Travels over all the inhabited earth. Inspections and reviews of an army of a million deranged minds. The mentally defective on the left, the over-gifted on the right. Foundation of research laboratories for exceptionally gifted animals" (*AF*, 464).

The restless activity of the mass-soul with its recurrent phantasms of unification testifies at the same time to the privatization of the collective life and the collective cultural creativity of the group. Canetti speaks of the "private myths" by which the novel figures are possessed, just as Freud speaks of individual neurosis as the last residue of collective beliefs.[25] The gorilla's creation of his own language, which dissolves the two rooms of his universe into a "magnetic field of passions" (*AF* 452), bears witness to the magmatic roots of creativity; this creativity manifests itself, however, as private myth, as madness, that is, as the negative truth of what Castoriadis calls "the always impossible and always realized coexistence of a private world (*kosmos idios*) and of a common or public world."[26] The mass-soul represents Canetti's first attempt to come to terms with his perception of this impossible coexistence, just as the novel as a whole sets out to present and diagnose the fate of the society of individuals through their individual-collective fantasies. The importance that Canetti attributes to the diagnostic significance of the *Memoirs* of Daniel Paul Schreber in *Crowds and Power* is in this sense a direct continuation of *Auto da Fé*. Schreber's grandiose delusional system is interpreted as the (private) "myth of the twentieth century," which documents the interplay of religion and politics (see chapter 3).

The mass-soul provides, as we have seen, the key to the negative dialectic of the individual. It accounts for the strange, inexplicable reversal of self-preservation into self-abandonment that befalls the individual as such, the closed personality, personified in Peter Kien. Peter, the man of stone, refuses openness to the other, that is to say, he refuses the possibility of transformation. His self-willed freezing into a granite statue to escape threatening life is the very antithesis of transformation. That is why his dreams are filled with alien and terrifying images of transformation, which form the prelude to his final surrender to fire, the most potent symbol of the irresistible power of the crowd. If Peter's surrender represents the catastrophic "solution" to the problem of individuation, it is because the possibility of transformation — Canetti's key to the open personality — lies beyond the reach of monadic closure. Peter's self-sacrifice is only the most extreme example. The "blind" beggar and Pfaff are also haunted by thoughts of suicide, while Therese and Fischerle's impulses towards self-transformation, animated by Peter Kien's money, remain on the level of daydreams.

> In his hiding place right at the back under the bed he counted over the beautiful new notes, just for the pleasure of it. He remembered exactly how many there were. As soon as he had done he started again at the beginning. Fischerle is off now to a far country, to America. (*AF,* 222)

Fischerle's imaginary new self, Dr. Siegfried Fischer, world chess champion and resident of the New World, falls victim to his Jewish self-hate. Seated before a mirror, he beats himself at chess and ends by hurling insults at his mirror image. Therese's moments of spontaneous feeling, in which she offers her imagined lovers her savings book, are just as rapidly dispelled by her ingrained possessiveness.

George, it seems, is the only figure open to genuine self-transformation. He owes his new life to his encounter with the gorilla. He is the opposite in every respect of Peter; the brothers' relationship is marked for this very reason by blindness. Peter asserts his unyielding character and dismisses his brother as a psychiatrist who plays with the sufferings of his patients and as an actor hungry for applause: "You poor creature, I'm sorry for you. The truth is you're a woman. You live for sensations. Let yourself go then, chase from one novelty to the next! I stand firm" (*AF,* 490). George in turn laments the "all-devouring lack of imagination in this Peter. A brain of lead, moulded out of letters, cold, rigid, heavy." If only he had the courage to murder his wife, "to sacrifice to his revenge manuscripts, texts, library, all the furniture of his lean heart" (*AF,* 505). Peter, he concludes, is nothing but an extinguished enigma. The very one-sidedness of the brothers, reflected in their mutual blindness and the impossibility of communication, underlines the negativity of each type, not only of the rigid character but also of the "selfless" fluidity of George's mimetic personality. The brothers appear in this light — but also of course Therese and Peter — as a satiric parody of Otto Weininger's categorical opposition of "gender" and "character," of the "feminine" and the "masculine" principles.[27] Peter traces all the evils of the world to the splitting of the sexes, the Fall of Man. In his eyes George embodies femininity, just as it is George, appropriately, who senses that their union would give rise to "universal man": "If you and I could be moulded together into a single being, the result would be a spiritually complete man" (*AF*, 490).

If George's universal man suggests a positive alternative to the negative dialectic of the individual, it indicates nothing more than an ideal counterpoint to the mass madness threatening the society of individuals, the (feared/ desired) destruction of civilization, which each of the brothers interprets in his own fashion. George compares it to a magnificent natural eruption of the utterly senseless; Peter is haunted by memories of a crime of legendary proportions, which demonstrates "how closely love and hatred are interwoven" (*AF*, 100). The brothers illustrate from opposite sides — nature and culture, crowds and power — the *auto-da-fé of civilization*. Peter's example comes from his speech to his books and is drawn appropriately from the land of civilization *par excellence,* the "Promised Land of all scholars," China:

> In the history of a certain country, a country honoured in equal measure by all of us here, a country in which you have yourselves been the object of the greatest respect, the most profound love, nay even of that religious veneration which is your due, in the history of this country, I say, one fearful event took place, a crime of legendary proportions, a crime perpetrated by a fiendish tyrant at the instigation of an adviser more fiendish than himself against you, my friends. In the year 213 before Christ, went out word from the Emperor of China, Shi Hoang Ti, a brutal usurper who had even dared to arrogate to himself the titles "the first, the auspicious, the godlike," that every book in China was to be burnt. (*AF*, 100–101)

George's example appropriately is that of a termite colony, since the "super organism" of insect societies, composed of millions of specialized units, perfectly fits his description of the mass as a "higher animal" (compare Hobbes' metaphor of the Leviathan). We may note here that Ernst Jünger presents his figure of the Worker (1932), conceived as the nemesis of the bourgeois society of individuals and inspired in equal measure by Spengler's "Prussian socialism" and Sorel's proletarian violence, as an irresistible amalgam of soldier and worker ants, that is, as "blind cells of a fanatic whole," in George's words. Jünger does not hesitate, moreover, to compare expressly and approvingly his coming Worker State to the senseless functioning of ant society.[28] The senselessness which seizes George's termite colony mirrors in reverse the madness that takes possession of the individual.

When they swarm, at which period thousands, nay millions, are destroyed apparently without reason, I see in this a release of the amassed sexuality of the stock. They sacrifice a part of their number, in order to preserve the rest from the aberration of love. The whole stock would run aground on this question of love, were it once to be permitted. I can imagine nothing more poignant than an orgy in a colony of termites. The creatures forget — a colossal recollection has seized hold of them — what they really are, the blind cells of a fanatic whole. Each will be himself, it begins with a hundred or a thousand of them, the madness spreads, *their* madness, a mass madness, the soldiers abandon the gates, the whole mound burns with unsatisfied love, they cannot find their partners, they have no sex, the noise, the excitement far greater than anything usual, attracts a storm of real ants; through the unguarded gates their deadly enemies press in, what soldier thinks of defending himself, they want only love; and the colony which might have lived for all eternity — that eternity for which we all long — dies, dies of love, dies of that urge through which we, mankind, prolong our existence! It is a sudden transformation of the wisest into the most foolish. It is — no, it can't be compared with anything — yes, it is as if by broad daylight, with healthy eyes and in full possession of your understanding, you were to set fire to yourself and all your books. (*AF*, 485–86)

What the brothers' examples have in common is the fusion of contraries, the con-fusion of Eros and Thanatos among the termites (as opposed to their strife in Freud's *Civilization and its Discontents*), of love and hatred in Peter's unification in death with his books. This fusion of contraries, whose medium and symbol is fire, sweeps away all the protecting walls separating inside and outside, head and world, culture and nature. Again, it is necessary to insist on the negativities of the novel: "world in the head" signifies the suicidal "redemption" of the head without world, that is to say, the madness which befalls the isolated monad, the *homo clausus*, seized like the termites by a colossal recollection, as deep as hunger or love, of a lost oneness of being. "World in the Head" completes and confirms the negative anthropology of the novel. And just as the negative anthropology of *Auto da Fé* points forward to *Crowds and Power*, so the missing countervailing human being, universal man, characterized by the capacity for *self-transformation* as opposed to the blind crowd-driven *reversals* of the figures in the novel, anticipates the promised but missing continuation of *Crowds and Power* (see chapter 4).

Life, Form, Transformation

In the first volume of *The Philosophy of Symbolic Forms* (1923) Ernst Cassirer, echoing Simmel's essay "The Conflict in Modern Culture" (1918), relates the task of philosophy of culture to what he sees as the fundamental antithesis of modern philosophy: the gulf between the original content of life and its representation, which defines the necessary destiny of culture.[29] And yet although the whole process of *Bildung* removes us further and further from the originality of life, there can be no turning back to the lost paradise of pure immediacy. Regression would be disastrous: the negation of symbolic forms leads not to the essence of "life" but to the destruction of culture. The unity of spirit can be attained only through giving the contents of life their true form, that is, through the transformation of life into spirit.[30] *Auto da Fé* reiterates Cassirer's warning against regression in apocalyptic fashion. The novel is directed, however, not only against the enemies of culture but equally against its defenders. The utter negativity of the novel's conclusion cuts off vitalist illusions, while insisting that the blindness of the "head" to the "world" springs from the gulf between "life" and its representation. What separates Canetti from Cassirer's philosophy of symbolic forms is not its reconstruction of the formative principles of myth, science and art, but Cassirer's belief in the evolutionary process of *Bildung*, which takes us from myth to science. As Hans Blumenberg has pointed out, Cassirer's *magnum opus* remains caught between a recognition of the autonomy of individual symbolic forms, such as myth, language, religion and art, and a (neo-Kantian) belief in science as the telos of the system as a whole.[31] Like Freud, Adorno, and Horkheimer, Canetti registers the interpenetration of the "archaic" and the "modern," barbarism and civilization, myth and enlightenment. What separates him in turn from their critiques of reason and defines the *differentia specifica* of his position is his adherence to a concept of reason that does not accept its division into the distinct spheres of myth, art, and science. The cognitive roots of Canetti's life-long quest to understand the enigma of human being and the social-historical lie in the sphere of pre-Socratic thought, prior to the differentiation of myth into art and science. It is precisely this refusal of analytic and theoretical differentiation that makes transformation such a central and at the same time unresolved concept in his work, not simply because its protean nature eludes determination but also because Canetti hesitated to the last to circumscribe and define it.

If we confine ourselves to the novel, transformation undoubtedly has the function of responding to the "fundamental antithesis" of modern culture: the split between life and forms. To understand the scope and range of transformation in the novel we must first clarify the relation between transformation, magma and the "mythical" conception of the world. Here Cassirer's analysis of transformation will help us to elucidate the mythical dimensions of the novel. Cassirer contrasts the polysynthetic mythical imagination with the analytic approach of science: "Whereas empirical thinking speaks of 'change' and seeks to understand it on the basis of a universal rule, mythical thinking knows only a simple metamorphosis (taken in the Ovidian, not the Goethean sense)."[32] Two distinct causalities are involved: in the case of science, force is understood as dissolving all reality into dynamic relations; in the case of myth force is tied to a material substance since mythical thought does not recognize the distinction between substance and force. We can therefore relate mythical thought, in particular the mythical conception of mana, which is prior to the division between substance and force and the psychical and the physical, to the magmatic ground of being and to the mass-soul. With its characteristic fluidity and merging of properties, mana provides the material substratum of the unity of life and the medium of its ceaseless transformations. The mythical sense of the totality of all living things, "within which each individual creature and thing is magically connected to the whole" (Cassirer, 194) underlies George's conception of the mass-soul, the longing — in Cassirer's words — "to burst through the barriers that separate him [the devotee of Tammuz, Attis or Dionysus] from the universe of living things, to intensify the life feeling in himself to the point of liberating himself from his generic or individual *particularity*" (188).

We can now distinguish between the types of transformation present in the novel. The return to the original source of life, the bursting of the barriers of individuation, defines the most extreme — total liberation — and the most deficient — total self-destruction — type of transformation. It results, as the *auto-da-fé* of civilization shows, in the annihilation of spirit. At the end of the novel there is no suggestion of resurrection, of rebirth from the ashes. Closely allied with this negativity is the *ambivalence* of transformation evident in the blind dynamic of reification and animation everywhere at work within the affective field of the novel figures. Thus Cassirer notes the simultaneous spiritualization and materialization of the cosmos in mythical thought (55). We have observed this ambivalence in relation to numbers and money, and to the library, the prime subject-object of transformations in the novel. Peter brings the library to life in imaginary dialogues, he mobilizes it into the serried ranks of his army, and it is as an anonymous crowd that the printed pages mutate into dancing letters and the books engulf him in cascades of blows. The fantasies of each of the figures are likewise characterized by reversals between living and "dead" matter, inflation and devaluation. Thus Peter is anguished by his dream of books turning again and again into human beings (*AF* 43–46); the imaginary millions that are to liberate Fischerle from his hump can be kept safe only by taking the place of his hump (*AF* 220). These "blind" transformations bear witness to the fearful dynamic inhabiting the society of individuals. And it is only against this imprisoned life of things that we can identify a positive conception of transformation as the (absent) alternative to the negative dialectic of the novel, and distinguish it from the gravitational pull of the "mass," the entropic dissolution of form, of spirit into an amorphous, ambivalent flux. Cassirer's definition of mythical transformation — "the change from one individual and concrete material form into another" (47) — can be directly related to George's image of universal man, since both signify the embrace and sublation of the polar tension between life and form. It is thus not by chance that Canetti sees the combination of fluidity and constancy as the key to the fascination of myth[33] and that this stylistic ideal characterizes both *Auto da Fé* and *Crowds and Power*. Canetti's realization that the world had fallen apart, that it could no longer be represented as in earlier novels, did not entail writing an incomprehensible and chaotic book. On the contrary, disciplined by the example of Stendhal's prose and by the years in the chemical laboratory working on his doctorate, he intended his novel to be a rigorous book, in which the sharply delineated figures were to stand out in their radical idiosyncrasy against the inchoate flux of the mass in all its ontological dimensions.[34] In comparable fashion the phenomenology of crowds and power seeks to transform conceptual analysis into "individual concrete and material form." "World in the Head" invites accordingly a double reading. As content, it presents the self-destructive revolt of imprisoned life (the mental asylum, the madness of Peter Kien, the gorilla in human clothes, George Kien's theory of the mass-soul); as formed content, by holding fast to the vision into the abyss, *Auto da Fé* fulfils Nietzsche's or Castoriadis's understanding of the function of great art: to open a window onto the chaos of Being and at the same time to give form to this chaos.

2: The Natural History of Modernity

E LIAS CANETTI'S *Crowds and Power* (1960) has been hailed by J. S. McClelland as the one masterpiece in the whole tradition of crowd theory since Plato (*CM*, 293). High praise indeed for a work which passes over this entire tradition in silence to develop a phenomenology and biology of crowds and power outside of the received categories of social psychology and political theory. It was thus a fellow-novelist, Saul Bellow, who summed up what no doubt many bewildered readers felt, when, in a thinly veiled reference to Canetti, in the guise of "this Bulgarian, Banowitch," his hero Herzog speaks of a "gruesome and crazy book": "Fairly inhuman and filled with vile paranoid hypotheses such as that crowds are fundamentally cannibalistic, that people standing secretly terrify the sitting, smiling teeth are the weapons of hunger, that the tyrant is mad for the sight of (possibly edible?) corpses about him." Nevertheless, Herzog must concede "that the making of corpses has been the most dramatic achievement of modern dictators and their followers (Hitler, Stalin, etc.)."[1] We can hardly be surprised that social scientists have kept their distance from a study which resists in such fashion theoretical appropriation. McClelland stands alone not only in his appraisal but even in his analysis of *Crowds and Power*. Serge Moscovici concludes his "historical treatise on mass psychology," *The Age of the Crowd*, with Freud and mentions Canetti only in passing. The reason for this is not simply historical. Moscovici is convinced that Freud solved the mystery of crowd psychology, all of whose elements had been assembled in popular and effective form by Gustave Le Bon. Freud's *Group Psychology and the Analysis of the Ego* (1921) is for Moscovici the one masterpiece of crowd theory.[2] Canetti's silence on Freud, along with Nietzsche, is particularly eloquent in *Crowds and Power*. He is not accorded the recognition of citation and appears only in the context of Canetti's analysis of Schreber's *Memoirs* in reference to "a well-known attempt to find the origins of his particular illness, and of paranoia in general, in repressed homosexuality," followed by the verdict: "There could scarcely, however, be a greater mistake" (*CP*, 522). There can be no doubt that in rejecting modern crowd theory since the French Revolution,

Canetti is seeking to displace *the psychological* interpretation of the crowd, which culminates in Freudian psychoanalysis, and which was already the target of his scorn in his novel *Auto da Fé,* written around 1930, thirty years before *Crowds and Power* was published.

For Canetti there cannot be two masterpieces of crowd theory. We can, however, accommodate both Moscovici and McClelland if we see Freud's study as the culmination and completion of crowd theory in the "age of the crowd," from the French Revolution to the First World War, governed at least since 1848 and above all since the Paris Commune by the bourgeoisie's fear of the urban masses. The First World War is, however, the watershed that separates the nineteenth-century age of the crowd from the twentieth-century age of totalitarianism. If Hitler was the leader crowd theory was waiting for, it is nevertheless clear that totalitarianism represents a new, historically unprecedented phenomenon, which challenged and exceeded the insights and fears of what we might call classical crowd theory. It is against the phenomenon and the theory of totalitarianism that we must situate and measure *Crowds and Power* and ask, whether in this light, it is in fact, as McClelland argues, the masterpiece that completes the whole tradition:

> The triumph of crowd politics with the rise of National Socialism in Germany enables Canetti to survey the *whole* experience of the crowd from its anthropological beginnings, and to re-work the whole tradition of crowd theory. In Canetti, crowd theory is completed in a sense that was not available to his predecessors, whose crowd theory could only be complete as prediction. In Canetti, the whole crowd experience itself *is* complete; the crowd and its leaders have come to power out of a decayed civilization. . . . (*CM*, 293)

Crowds and Power is connected with and separated from its predecessors in a double fashion: first, by the intention to re-work the whole tradition of crowd theory *ab initio;* second, by seeking to comprehend thereby the new phenomenon of totalitarianism, manifested in the triumph of crowd politics in National Socialism. My interest is this second determining focus of *Crowds and Power.* Clearly, however, it cannot be addressed without first recalling the main elements of nineteenth century crowd theory. Here, I follow Moscovici's reconstruction of the new science of mass psychology, which responded to the emergence of "the masses" since the French Revolution.[3]

Moscovici discerns three initial answers to the question of the crowd: (1) the crowd comprises the asocial mass of individuals on the fringes of society — the mob, the rabble, the lumpenproletariat; (2) the crowd is insane, unbridled, hysterical, the manifestation of the psychological abnormality of collective behavior; (3) the crowd is criminal, given to blind violence, its study a branch of "criminal anthropology" (Lombroso) — an attitude extended by Scipio Sighele to include all kinds of social movements and political groups from anarchists to socialists. The view of the crowd as criminally abnormal, that is, external to society and thus a matter for the police, was challenged and transformed by Gustave Le Bon. The crowd can be anybody and everybody, since the decisive characteristic of crowds is their fusion of individuals into a common mind or emotion that dissolves personal and class distinctions. As a member of the crowd the individual feels, thinks and behaves differently, he moves "in a different mental universe with its own peculiar logic." This means that the crowd has an autonomous status, which is not external to society; on the contrary, it is the supreme activity of communal existence, which reveals the power of the collectivity underlying and concealed by society's official institutions. Just as the crowd dissolves individual distinctions, so we could think of the crowd since the French Revolution as the manifestation of the instituting energy of the collectivity (Canetti's open crowds) which negates and threatens to dissolve the instituted power, classes and organized groups of society (Tarde and Freud's artificial crowds, Canetti's closed crowds).

The problem for mass psychology thus lies in the riddle of crowd formation, the metamorphosis of the socialized individual in the crowd, characterized on the one hand by a lowering of intellectual faculties and the intensification of emotional reactions, on the other by the suspension of self-interest and self-preservation, resulting in behavior equally capable of destructive fury and of selfless heroism. Altruism, blind devotion, self-abnegation and sacrifice are for Le Bon collective virtues. Individual and mass psychology thus stand sharply opposed. The economic self-interest and the self-preserving reason of the individual are cancelled in the irrational behavior of the crowd. For an explanation of this mysterious metamorphosis, Gabriel Tarde and Le Bon turned to French psychology and its central concern in the 1880s and 1890s: hypnosis. The power of suggestion, evinced in hypnosis, could be applied to mass psychology: individuals in a crowd behave as if hypnotized, and it is this which explains the power of the leader over the crowd. Propaganda's methods of collective suggestion replace the rhetoric of political persuasion. And here we should add, if we follow the model of hypnosis, that propaganda is to be thought of as a command disguised as suggestion, an unconscious command.

Moscovici stresses that the originality of mass psychology lies in its affirmation before Freud of the power of the unconscious. But although pre-

Freudian theorists understood that crowd psychology was the psychology of the unconscious, it was still left to Freud to propose an alternative to the hypothesis of hypnotic suggestion. In the process Freud completed the implications of the hypnotic model: the transformation of the psychology of the crowd into the psychology of the *leader*,[4] even though Freud's interest is the artificial crowd (the church, the army) as opposed to the natural or spontaneous crowd.

Freud explained suggestion in terms of the erotic bonds which unite the crowd, replacing individual narcissistic libido. The renunciation of self-love leads to submission to and identification with the leader, who alone is governed by self-love. The crowd identifies with itself in and through the leader: "In crowd psychology, the leader is the common element, the universal and indispensable super-ego and social ego around which men unite."[5] Moscovici compares Freud's and Canetti's understanding of the unity and equality of the crowd. For Canetti the *discharge is* the most important occurrence within the crowd: "Before this the crowd does not actually exist; it is the discharge which creates it. This is the moment when all who belong to the crowd get rid of their differences and feel equal" (*CP*, 19). The full significance of this understanding of the crowd only appears when it is seen as Canetti's response to Freud and to the foregoing crowd theory. Freud writes in *Group Psychology:* "Do not let us forget, however, that the demand for equality in a group applies only to its members and not to the leader. All the members must be equal to one another, but they all want to be ruled by one person."[6]

The question that crowd theory hands on to totalitarian theory, and that appears most clearly in fascism, is that of the relation between the crowd and the leader, that is, the relation between crowds and power. Bearing this question in mind, I want to approach *Crowds and Power* not only through a comparison with crowd theory, as does McClelland, but also through a juxtaposition with the theories of totalitarianism advanced by Theodor Adorno (b. 1903) and Hannah Arendt (b. 1906), the exact contemporaries of Canetti (b. 1905), and like him decisively shaped by the experience of the rise of National Socialism.[7]

Dialectic of Enlightenment

In the introduction to *Dialectic of Enlightenment* (1944) Horkheimer and Adorno speak of the "enigmatic readiness of the technologically educated masses to fall under the sway of any despotism" and of the masses' "self-destructive affinity to popular [völkisch] paranoia," in all its uncom-prehended absurdity, as the challenge to self-reflective thought (*DE*, xiii). Crowds and their leaders play, however, only a secondary role in their analy-ses of the self-destruction of enlightenment. They have mutated into the interchangeable units of mass society:

> The modern fascist bosses are not so much supermen as functions of their own propaganda machine, the focal points at which identical re-actions of countless citizens intersect. In the psychology of the modern masses, the Führer is not so much a father-figure as a collective and over-exaggerated projection of the powerless ego of each individual to which the so-called "leaders" in fact correspond. . . . Part of their moral influence consists precisely in the fact that they are powerless in them-selves but deputize for all other powerless individuals, and embody the fullness of power for them, without themselves being anything other than the vacant spaces taken up accidentally by power. (*DE*, 236)

Crowds and their leaders have become powerless functions of power. More exactly, the visible face of power, the focal point of mass projection, is a vacant space. Both crowds and power are subsumed by the "invisible power" (*DE*, 10) of domination. It is in this sense that the truth of the bourgeois system of order appears in naked form in fascism (*DE*, 170), and that it represents the culmination of the "unconditional realism of civi-lized humanity" (*DE*, 193). The new phenomenon of totalitarianism is thus comprehended in its genealogy. It is a genealogy, however, which cannot distinguish between the logic of calculating reason, under whose light the new barbarism grows to fruition (*DE*, 32), and the manifest irrationality of a triumphant fascism, because the one is the truth of the other. The "mass paranoia" (*DE*, 196) of fascism is already contained in the "paranoiac delusion" (*DE*, 193) of civilized humanity, the unconditional realism of objectifying thought.

This means that the "psychology of the modern masses" in its col-lective self-projection is itself like its leaders a vacant space, through which we glimpse — not, with Freud, the primal horde, blindly obedient to its despotic chief, the "superman" at the very beginning of the history of mankind, but the original history of a subjectivity that constituted itself as a vacant space, as a Nobody, between the Scylla of nature and the Charybdis of domination. Mass psychology appears literally to explain nothing. The masses and their leader are no more than epiphenomena, and yet, although Horkheimer and Adorno expressly distance themselves from Freud's father figure, the very model of the dialectic of enlightenment is to be found in Freud's dialectic of civilization. That is to say, the underlying narrative or myth of *Dialectic of Enlightenment* is that of natural history, which, like Freud's essays into social psychology and the (pre-)history of civilization, excludes the social and political domain (the domain of power proper), to read in civilization and in modernity the pattern of the archaic. Natural history can dispense with mass psychology, even if paranoia is the key to anti-Semitism, because natural history is psychology writ large: "the curse of irresistible progress is irresistible regression" (*DE*, 36). Nature (the id) and domination (the super-ego) act in the blind unconscious collusion of a self-reinforcing dynamic of repression, which finally liquidates in the masses of mass society even the illusion of the ego's autonomy. Natural history requires no human agency; it is not a theory of action but a theory of systematic, that is, unconsciously operating, power.[8]

Crowds and power are replaced by paranoia and domination in *Dialectic of Enlightenment*. Natural history tells the story of origins and totalitarian conclusions in relation to both domination and paranoia, the two mythical accounts of enlightenment that we must now examine more closely.

The mythical account of enlightenment is summed up in the double thesis: "myth is already enlightenment: and enlightenment reverts to mythology" (*DE*, xvi). The dialectic of enlightenment unfolds the story of a self-destructive self-preservation whose origin and dynamic are dictated by the imperative: dominate that you be not dominated. "The essence of enlightenment is the alternative whose ineradicability is that of domination. Men have always had to choose between their subjection to nature or the subjection of nature to the Self" (*DE*, 32). This self is the self of self-preservation, the self that is called upon to sacrifice itself in order to survive. This dialectic, which contains the origin of the individual, of subjectivity, of enlightenment, already foreshadows the totalitarian reversion of the individual to the collective. The dialectic of enlightenment thus enacts the dialectic of civilization as defined by Freud: given the crushingly superior force of nature, "the principal task of civilization, its actual *raison d'être*, is to defend us against nature."[9] Horkheimer and Adorno radicalize Freud's open-ended dialectic. The return of the repressed is the inescapable consequence of the escape from nature's domination: "society continues threatening nature as the lasting, organized compulsion which is reproduced in individuals as rational self-preservation . . ." (*DE*, 181). Freud's founding myth of civilization, and of the individual, the myth of Oedipus, is replaced by the myth of the escape from myth, the myth of Odysseus. The difference between the two myths is obvious. The place of the Father has become a vacant space; Adorno and Horkheimer are not interested in the psychology of the leader. The similarities, however, are of greater importance. Both myths relate from opposite sides the perils of the regression to mother nature: "The dread of losing the self and of abrogating together with the self the barrier between oneself and the other life, the fear of death and destruction, is intimately associated with a promise of happiness which threatened civilization at every moment" (*DE*, 33). If enlightenment is the very principle of myth, it is because enlightenment is mythic fear turned radical (*DE*, 16).

Since for Horkheimer and Adorno self-preservation is the ultimate context and the true maxim of Western civilization (*DE*, 29), we could also say that the history of civilization functions as the bridge and the interregnum between the archaic and the modern, between the beginnings and the end of the individual. The natural history of civilization — the domination of nature by man — unfolds "the evolutionary law of society, the principle of self" (*DE*, 36). It is this and not the psychology of the modern masses that provides the key to their enigmatic surrender to despotic leaders. The enigma of the masses — the suspension of self-interest, the abandonment of self-preservation — is to be explained by the very principle of self-preservation. On one level, it is clear, the masses are the victims of power, the victims of the wholesale deception practiced by enlightenment in the service of power (*DE*, 42). But on a deeper level, it is clear, the masses in their powerlessness are unconsciously complicit in their fate, since the price of self-preservation is identification with power, which was always the power of the collective: "What is done to all by the few, always occurs as the subjection of individuals by the many: social repression always exhibits the masks of repression by a collective" (*DE*, 22). Liberation from "natural thralldom" only leads ever more deeply into "natural enslavement," that is, into self-enslavement: "Hence the course of European civilization" (*DE*, 13). This is the message of the founding myth of self-preservation: "Only he who submits survives in the face of the gods. The awakening of the self is paid for by the acknowledgment of power as the principle of all relations" (*DE*, 9).

Behind the domination of nature in the service of self-preservation "lurks the latent phantasm of total power,"[10] and what it reveals in naked form in fascism is that self-preservation always demanded self-sacrificing submission to domination. The systemic organization and rational integration of power, whose origin is mythic terror, ends in terroristic myth. Totalitarianism, in the most general sense of "the development to total integration" (*DE*, x), returns men to a state of nature, "once again made to be . . . mere species beings, exactly like one another through isolation in the forcibly united collectivity" (*DE,* 36). Here we can see how totalitarian theory diverges from crowd theory. Totalitarian theory replaces the crowd by the masses (allowing for the ambiguity of the German where the two terms are covered by the one word — *die Masse).* In crowd theory the eruption of the crowd within each of us signals the return of the repressed, which threatens all the institutions of civilization. For Horkheimer and Adorno the threat comes not from the anarchic crowd but from the repressive collective within each of us. Indeed, fascism "is also totalitarian in that it seeks to make the rebellion of suppressed nature against domination directly useful to domination" (*DE,* 185). The disintegration of the bourgeois individual in mass society is equally cause and effect of his integration into the barbaric collective.

Thus Horkheimer and Adorno believe, unlike Canetti, that crowds cannot present a counter-principle to power. Moreover, paranoia is not the "illness of power" (Canetti), the key to the psychology of the leader, so much as the sickness of the atomized masses, who find in anti-Semitism the compensation for their impotence: "the hatred felt by the led . . . knows no bounds" (*DE,* 171). Paranoia derives from self-preservation. Its genealogy is also that of natural history, of the archaic in the modern, of the ambivalence of the origin and its return in totally perverted form. At the beginning (which, as we shall see, is also the beginning for Canetti) stands the dread and attraction of the return to nature: the fear of death and destruction which is "intimately associated with a promise of happiness" (*DE,* 33). At the end stands the repressed longing permitted only as hatred: "even hatred leads to unification with the object — in destruction" (*DE,* 199). The paranoiac pathology of projection, which no longer recognizes the difference between the inner and the outer world, is driven by the vain attempt to overcome the intolerable gulf "between individual fate and social law" (*DE,* 196), which renders the individual meaningless. In this sense paranoia mimics the immediacy of original mimesis, just as totalitarian movements promise the immediacy of equality in the one people or the one class, achieved once they have seized power by the equalizing force of terror.

The return to a state of nature in totalitarianism ratifies the dialectic of civilization: "the victory of society over nature which changes everything into pure nature" (*DE,* 186). If paranoiac projection is to be understood as a pathology of cognition, the manifestation of the "dark side of cognition" (*DE,* 195), it is because cognition is rooted in nature, rooted in what Canetti calls "the entrails of power." The beginning and the end of cognition are encompassed by mimesis and paranoia, the two immediate, concrete forms of incorporation by the object and the subject respectively:

> Anti-Semitism is based on a false projection. It is the counterpart of true mimesis, and fundamentally related to the repressed form; in fact, it is probably the morbid expression of repressed mimesis. Mimesis imitates the environment, but false projection makes the environment like itself. (*DE,* 187)

Here we must recall the ambivalence of mimesis. It is on the one hand the *chiffre* of reconciliation with nature, horrifyingly negated and parodied in "the unification with the object — in destruction." On the other hand, the immediacy of mimesis is that of the original state of terror from which civilization sought to escape, the "moments of biological prehistory," the "approximation to death for the sake of survival" (*DE,* 180–81).

> Civilization has replaced the organic adaptation to others and mimetic behaviour proper, by organized control of mimesis, in the magical phase; and finally, by rational practice, by work, in the historical phase. (*DE,* 180)

Whether magical or rational, cognition remains attached to the original state of terror in its reversal of mimesis: "The *ratio* which supplants mimesis is not simply its counterpart. It is itself mimesis: mimesis unto death" (*DE,* 57). The fear of incorporation (for Canetti the source of "the oldest terrors") is transformed into the incorporating power of cognition, whose functions of "persecuting, fixing, and seizing" have been "intellectualized from the primitive suppression of the animal nature into scientific methods of controlling nature" (*DE,* 193). Behind the abstract power of the reifying concept lurks the violence that makes the environment like itself. The *ratio's* deadly mimesis must thus be grasped concretely as the triumph of death-in-life, whose ultimate logic is revealed in the life-in-death of paranoiac destruction. In the death camps, it is "death which stands up and lives" (*DE,* 235).

The ambivalence of mimesis points to the two natural histories of civilization traced in *Dialectic of Enlightenment.* The one evokes the negation of domination, carried by the remembrance of nature in the subject, "in whose fulfilment the unacknowledged truth of all culture lies hidden" (*DE,* 40). The other relates the natural history of domination as the undeniable truth of all culture, which is laid bare in fascist totalitarianism. The two dimensions of domination that we have analyzed — self-preservation and paranoia — belong together, for in paranoia we must recognize the "isolated pattern of self-preservation" (*DE,* 195). This isolated pattern is particularly relevant to the psychology of mass society, where the "asocial forms" (Freud) of neurosis reflect the isolation of the individual from the collectivity of systems of faith. The modern neurotic individual is the individual rendered meaningless, driven by *horror vacui* to embrace the collective paranoia celebrated in fascist ideology (*DE*, 196–97).

Crowds and Power

Nietzsche and Freud, the unmaskers of the Enlightenment's illusions, are central to Adorno and Horkheimer's genealogy of power and dialectic of civilization. They are the silent adversaries of Canetti. The reckoning with Nietzsche's "will to power" is reserved for *Crowds and Power*. The rejection of psychoanalysis, fueled by Canetti's encounter with and direct experience of the crowd, is already the driving impulse of his early novel, *Auto da Fé*. The debate with Freud and the critique of crowd theory remains of course central to *Crowds and Power*. A clarification of the differences between Canetti and Freud will lead us into the central concerns of Canetti's study.

In *Group Psychology and the Analysis of the Ego,* Freud explores the relation between individual and group psychology. The crucial section for our purposes is "The Group and the Primal Horde," where Freud takes up the argument already advanced in *Totem and Taboo,* namely the speculative development of Darwin's conjecture that "the primitive form of human society was that of a "horde ruled over despotically by a powerful male" (*GP,* 154). Freud argues that the key to the psychology of the crowd is to be found in the primal horde:

> Just as primitive man survives potentially in every individual, so the primal horde may arise once more out of any random collection; in so far as men are habitually under the sway of group formation we recognize in it the survival of the primal horde. We must conclude that the psychology of groups is the oldest human psychology; what we have isolated as individual psychology has only come into prominence out of the old group psychology. . . . (*GP,* 155)

The crucial word here is "isolated": just as the individual emerges from and progressively isolates himself from the group (the horde, the clan, the social collectivity), so comparably individual psychology is obtained by a process of isolation: individual psychology is group psychology isolated. The implication of Freud's conclusion only appears when we reverse the intention of his argument: if the primal horde offers the key to the psychology of the crowd, then we are equally entitled to argue that the psychology of the crowd offers the key to individual psychology. That Freud both did and did not draw this conclusion is evident from the disjunction between the scientific teachings of psychoanalysis and the "scientific myth" of his speculations on civilization, which have remained an embarrassing foreign body for the psychoanalytic movement.

Freud states that there is one psychology, group psychology, of which individual psychology is a derivative. As we have seen, Horkheimer and Adorno follow Freud in his explanation of *individual* neurosis as a consequence of the loss of the powerful protection afforded by the *collective* neurosis of religious illusions. "If he is left to himself, a neurotic is obliged to replace by his own symptom formations the great group formations from which he is excluded. He creates his own world of the imagination for himself, his own religion, his own system of delusions, and thus recapitulates the institutions of humanity in a distorted way . . ." (*GP,* 176). Individual neurosis isolates; more exactly, the individual qua individual, isolated from the group, is neurotic *per se* — unless he is a leader. There is in fact not just one psychology. There are two. If group psychology offers the key to the analysis of the ego, this is the case only because there is a leader: "It is impossible to grasp the nature of the group if the leader is disregarded" (*GP,* 150). Thus Freud immediately corrects the statement that group psychology is the oldest human psychology: "Individual psychology must, on the contrary, be just as old as group psychology, for from the first there were two kinds of psychologies, that of individual members of the group and that of the father, chief, or leader" (*GP,* 155).

With this original, primary distinction between the leader and the led, between the horde, the crowd, mass man, and the superman, Freud's speculations, which departed from Darwin, find their point of arrival in Nietzsche. What is the psychology of the leader as opposed to the crippled animal of civilization?

> The members of the group were subject to ties just as we see them today, but the father of the primal horde was free. His intellectual acts were strong and independent even in isolation, and his will needed no reinforcement from others. Consistency leads us to assume that his ego had few libidinal ties; he loved no one but himself, or other people only in so far as they served his needs. . . . He, at the very beginning of the history of mankind, was the "superman," whom Nietzsche only expected from the future. (*GP,* 155)

Here in the two kinds of psychologies we have Freud's version of crowds and power. The psychology of the crowd (crowd theory) and the psychology of power (the Nietzschean superman), brought together by Freud, are the two enemies that Canetti confronts. What Freud has brought together must be torn asunder. There are two kinds of psychologies in *Crowds and Power*, but they no longer manifest the "natural" complementarity of the leader and the led. Crowds and power are irreducible principles, which are "naturally" antagonistic. This insistence on two principles sharply distinguishes *Crowds and Power* from Horkheimer and Adorno's *dialectic* of domination and consequent inescapable closure of history. Domination is for Canetti only the one side of an undecided history, and in this sense we can observe a certain affinity between Canetti's opposition of crowds and power and Freud's open-ended struggle between Eros and Thanatos, the instinct of life and the instinct of destruction (allowing for Canetti's resolute rejection of Freud's death drive). At the very time Freud was writing in *Civilization and its Discontents* — "civilization is a process in the service of Eros, whose purpose is to combine single human individuals, and after that families, then races, peoples and nations, into one great unity, the unity of mankind. Why this has to happen we do not know; the work of Eros is precisely this"[11] — Canetti is setting forth in *Auto da Fé* his theory of the crowd, which culminates in the vision of its future global triumph: "There will come a time when it is not scattered again, possibly in a single country at first, eating its way out from there, until no one can doubt any more, for there will be no I, you, he, but only it, the mass."

Canetti gave his novel the title *Die Blendung* — blinding, dazzlement, deception. It signifies the blindness of the individual to the crowd within, the blindness of individual psychology to "that far deeper and most special motive force of history, the desire of men to rise into a higher type of animal, into the mass, and to lose themselves in it so completely as to forget that one man ever existed, . . ." The discovery of the "effects of the mass on history in general and on the life of individuals" appears at first sight to be an enthusiastic recapitulation of crowd theory:

> We wage the so-called war of existence for the destruction of the mass-soul in ourselves, no less than for hunger and love. In certain circumstances it can become so strong as to force the individual to selfless acts or even acts contrary to their own interests. "Mankind" has existed as a mass for long before it was conceived of and watered down into an idea. (*AF*, 461)

In fact, however, the very closeness of George Kien's conception of the mass-soul to received theory hides the radical reversal at work here, which completes the implication of Freud's ego analysis and turns it against crowd theory itself. Moscovici sums up crowd theory's solution to the riddle of crowd behavior in the formula: *"crowds are the unconscious.* Thus crowd psychology is simultaneously the psychology of the unconscious."[12] Canetti reverses the received truth in the most direct and most simple fashion: the crowd is not the unconscious, on the contrary, *the unconscious is the crowd,* the crowd within the individual. "Countless people go mad because the mass in them is particularly strongly developed and can get no satisfaction" (*AF,* 462).[13]

This reversal makes *Auto da Fé* the exemplification of Freud's own "crowd" interpretation of individual neurosis, quoted above. The isolated neurotic, compelled to create his own religion, his own system of delusions, becomes in Canetti's novel the atomized individual of mass society, "poor, lonely devils," each imprisoned in the monadic isolation of his private myth. (As we shall see in the next chapter, in *Crowds and Power* Canetti links the history of the crowd closely with the history of religions.) And this private myth, which takes the place of the "great group formations" of history, is nothing other for Canetti than the expression of the *crowd in the head,* the crowd within, which cannot be killed and returns in the mad distorted guise of a private religion, characterized by images of increase (money, books, adoring masses) and the inflation of the self, that is, by fantasies of crowds and power. *Auto da Fé* thus already contains the two kinds of psychologies that are the subject of *Crowds and Power.* In contrast to Freud's two psychologies, that of the horde and that of the leader, where the psychology of the leader explains that of the crowd (cf. *GP,* 153), here we have the primacy of the crowd, which explains the psychology of the isolated individual held fast in the blindness of self-preservation, behind which lurks, as for Horkheimer and Adorno, the phantasm of total power. For Canetti, the problem lies not in the crowd but in the individual, that is, in the very principle of individuation.[14]

McClelland aptly calls Canetti the first autobiographer of the crowd (*CM,* 294). The starting point of *Crowds and Power* is the experience of the crowd from within, the moment of the reversal of the fear of being touched through contact with and surrender to the crowd: "suddenly it is as though everything were happening in one and the same body" (*CP,* 16). The significance of this reversal cannot be overestimated; it is simultaneously the surrender to and the liberation from the "oldest terrors" of animal life, the fear of seizure and incorporation: "We dream of it, we imagine it, and civilized life is nothing but a sustained effort to avoid it" (*CP,* 238). It is this fear which creates the boundaries of the personality, all the distances and hierarchies of society. Man, however, "petrifies and darkens in the distances he has created" and longs for liberation. Alone he cannot free himself, "only together can men free themselves from their burdens of distance," and this is what is achieved in the discharge: "the moment when all who belong to the crowd get rid of their differences and feel equal." "It is for the sake of this blessed moment, when no one is greater or better than another, that people become a crowd" (*CP*, 18–19).

The crowd for Canetti is a "mysterious and universal phenomenon" (*CP*, 16):

> The crowd is the same everywhere, in all periods and cultures; it remains essentially the same among men of the most diverse origin, education and language. Once in being, it spreads with the utmost violence. Few can resist its contagion; it always wants to go on growing and there are no inherent limits to its growth. It can arise, wherever people are to-gether, and its spontaneity and suddenness are uncanny. (*CP*, 89)

The essential quality of the natural or open crowd is the urge to grow: it "wants to seize everyone within reach" (*CP*, 17); its hunger cannot be satiated. "One cannot be certain whether this hunger would persist once it had really absorbed all men, but it seems likely" (*CP*, 24). A crowd which is not increasing is in a "state of fast" (*CP*, 26). The natural crowd thus has two essential dimensions: the liberation from the burden of individuation in the discharge which constitutes the crowd, and the crowd's hunger for increase, which knows no limits and seeks to destroy all barriers to its growth.

If the moment of equality is the moment of the crowd, "the moment of *survival* is the moment of power" (*CP*, 265). Here the equality of all is replaced by the struggle in which "each man is the enemy of every other." In-stead of the liberation from individuation, we have the survivor's feeling of uniqueness, the "elemental triumph" of survival. "Death has been deflected from him to those others" (*CP*, 266). Survival is Canetti's concept for the instinct of self-preservation: "True, he [man] wants to 'preserve' himself, but he also wants other things which are inseparable from this. He wants to kill so that he can survive others; he wants to stay alive so as not to have others sur-viving him" (*CP*, 293). We are all survivors — "The wish to see death is every-where and one does not have to go deep into men to bring it to light" (*CP*, 84),[15] but in those who command power, survival can become a "dangerous and insatiable passion," which feeds on its own increase (*CP*, 268). The essence of power, which is "sufficient unto itself and wills only itself" (*CP*, 241), is the power over life and death, that is, the power of death, deflected onto others.

The hunger of the crowd is never saturated, the passion for survival is insatiable. The metaphors of eating — people are the food of the crowd and of power — are meant literally: "Everything which is eaten is the food of power" (*CP*, 257). The process of eating, of assimilation into the body of the eater, embodies for Canetti the central, most hidden, process of power (*CP*, 246), revealed in the ultimate aim of the ruler over men: "to incorporate them into himself and to suck the substance out of them" (*CP*, 245). The biology of the crowd and the biology of power are the same: each lives and feeds its urge to grow through seizing and incorporating.

The parallelism between the biology of the crowd and of power points in two directions. On the one hand, it reveals the crowd as a destructive phenomenon, as its primary symbol, fire, indicates. On the other hand, the difference between their respective drives to escape death make the crowd and power distinct principles, as opposed to Horkheimer and Adorno's single logic of self-preservation and domination. For Canetti too self-preservation is governed by the deadly logic of either/or and for him too the origin of power *and* the crowd derives from the reversal of the "oldest terrors," the "moments of biological prehistory," the mimetic "approximation to death for the sake of survival" (*DE*, 180, 181). The one reversal is the moment of individual *survival,* the other is the moment of *equality* in the crowd, that is to say, a form of survival in which the self and self-preserving domination, driven by the fear of seizure and incorporation, are abandoned and transcended. Through incorporation into the crowd the individual is liberated from the fear of death and its logic of domination. The moment of the crowd must be understood in the fullest sense as the experience of *the sublime,* the transcendence of the boundaries of the personality through the surrender to death which breaks the taboo of civilization — regression, to extinguish all social differences in the return to a state of equality. Since it embodies the transcendence of death, the one body of the crowd both realizes and reverses the mythic fear of enlightenment: "The dread of losing the self and of abrogating together with the self the barrier between oneself and other life, the fear of death and destruction, is intimately associated with a promise of happiness which threatened civilization in every moment" (*DE*, 33).

The natural crowd and power are presented as biological *Urphäno-mene.* Nevertheless, they were preceded for many thousands of years before agriculture and the emergence and formation of the state by the pack,

Canetti's (animal) term for the "usual concepts of tribe, sib, clan" (*CP*, 111). The pack is an embryonic crowd that cannot grow and replaces growth by, for instance, the totemic religion of increase. The pack in its various forms contains in nucleus not only the behavior of crowds but also the germ of the various world religions (see his chapter "The Pack and Religion"). The close relationship between crowds and universal religions allows us to construct a schematic account of the genealogy of the crowd and of power in modernity:

(1) social units before the existence of the state: in the long period of prehistory there is no separation between the *pack* and power;

(2) the stratified state: the separation of crowds and power is mediated by the *closed crowds* of religion. Both the closed crowd and power are heteronomous, defined by their relationship to an instituting Other;[16]

(3) the modern state: since the French Revolution and the disintegration of the containing and taming power of religion, the crowd emerges in open opposition to the state and inaugurates political modernity. The *open crowd* and power are now autonomous, no longer defined by relation to a transcendent Other.

This is not an evolutionary history, conceived as progress — or as Spenglerian downfall. On the contrary, philosophy of history is replaced by natural history. In contrast to Horkeimer and Adorno's version of natural history, but comparable, as we shall see, to Arendt's version, Canetti presents a paradoxical natural history of civilization, in which the crowd and of power emerge in their naked, biological form in modernity after the death of transcendence, to reveal in their autonomy the two faces as it were of the Nietzschean will to power. Thus Canetti writes of the crowd since the French Revolution:

> To an impressive degree the crowd has freed itself from the substance of traditional religion and this has perhaps made it easier for us to see it in its nakedness, in what one might call its biological state, without the transcendental theories and goals which used to be inculcated in it. The history of the last 150 years has culminated in a spate of such eruptions; they have engulfed even wars, for all wars are now mass wars. The crowd is no longer content with pious promises and conditionals. It wants to experience for itself the strongest possible feeling of its own animal force and passion and, as means to this end, it will use whatever social pretexts and demands offer themselves. (*CP*, 23)

These eruptions of the modern crowd are the direct consequence of the accelerating growth of population and of cities, which can no longer be contained within the closed crowds of the past (*CP*, 22). Clearly this also involves a correlation between the growth of the crowd and the concentration of power — if crowds feed on people, the demagogue and despot feeds on crowds.[17] But it is also clear that the sublime moment of the revolutionary crowd and the unchaining of despotic power each reflect the loss of transcendence, the loss of the instituting Other which contained the crowd and in legitimating limited the absolute power of the ruler. If the revolutionary crowd embodies the immanence of the instituting power of society, that is, the abyss of foundation, as Marc Richir argues,[18] it is because, in Canetti's terms, modernity was born from the reversal crowds of the French Revolution. As we have seen, the natural crowd as such entails an act of reversal — the escape from the logic of self-preservation and domination — but the reversal crowd proper has as its goal the overthrow of the source of "*all* commands" (*CP*, 382), whose power derives from what Richir calls the infinite debt of death. "God himself has suspended the sentence of death over all living men . . ." (*CP*, 271), and from it flows the instituted power of the ruler. The sublime instituting power of the revolutionary crowd comes from the liberation from death's domination. The sentence of death is proclaimed over the death-sentence, personified in the monarch, God's deputy (*CP*, 382). The revolutionary act of foundation initiates, however, a deadly dialectic. The symbolic execution of God enthrones the absolute power of death, and when death becomes absolute (the meaning and measure of the individual), power becomes unlimited. It is precisely in this sense that we can say that the French Revolution is the origin of the natural history of modernity. The Revolution reveals in crowds and power its Janus face — the recovery of the golden age of equality, but also the terror, in which the Revolution devours its children.

The sentence of death suspended over all living men signifies for Canetti the ultimate *raison d'être* of the crowd and of power, conceived as the opposite extremes of the attempt to escape the fear of death that defines the individual. "The worst that can happen to men in war is to perish together; and this spares them death as individuals, which is what they fear most" (*CP*, 84). The crowd and power both act as deflectors of death: "The threat of death hangs over all men . . . it affects them all the time and creates in them the need to deflect death onto others" (*CP*, 56). Here again we see why only the strict separation of crowds and power enables Canetti to escape Horkheimer and Adorno's fatal dialectic of domination. This strict separation poses, however, a fundamental question: can it be maintained in the face of the apparent symbiosis between crowds and power, the masses and their leaders in totalitarianism?

McClelland makes a strong case for Canetti's position. Indeed, he sees in Canetti's assertion of the autonomy of the crowd, which renders it immune to the power of command ("the self-delusions of demagogues notwithstanding" (*CM*, 333) the key to the unraveling of the whole tradition of crowd theory in *Crowds and Power*. Even given the fact that "some of history's most lethal crowds have had particularly murderous leaders" (*CM*, 333), Canetti's achievement nevertheless lies in "the theoretical separation between the power of leaders and the crowd," which alone can overcome the consistent misunderstanding of the crowd in crowd theory since Plato (*CM*, 334). The true originality of Canetti emerges in hindsight — on the one hand, crowd theory "failed to provide a convincing psychopathology of power" (*CM*, 314); on the other hand, it failed to envisage the crowd as victims of power, even though McClelland concedes that "Canetti has to tread carefully here because the crowd has connived at all the twentieth century's great disasters" (*CM*, 311). The result, however, is that Canetti treads so carefully that he never actually confronts the question of the connection between crowds and power, posed so directly by the rise of Hitler, but chooses rather to approach it indirectly first from the side of the crowd and then of power. The dynamic of crowd politics in Germany, traced by Canetti in the sections "Germany and Versailles" and "Inflation and the Crowd," is well summarized by McClelland:

> In the Hitler case, the crowd crystal is the party faithful; the Party at large was recruited from the open crowd which formed when the closed crowd of the army erupted into the nation after the Treaty of Versailles; the inflation divided Germany into two crowds, the degraded flight crowd and the degraded crowd of Jews on to whom the inflation crowd transferred its own sense of worthlessness it felt in the devaluation of its money; . . . the degraded Jews became the crowd of hostile bacilli fit only for extermination; . . . and all the time Hitler as the leader-survivor intended to survive even larger numbers than he had survived in the First World War. (*CM*, 321)

Canetti places the conception of National Socialism at the moment of the outbreak of war in 1914. This was Hitler's decisive experience, "the one moment at which he himself honestly became part of the crowd. He never forgot it and his whole subsequent career was devoted to the re-creation of this moment, but *from outside*" (*CP*, 211). But Canetti does not tell us what gave Hitler power over the crowd, while McClelland's answer in his chapter on Hitler appears to contradict his own reading of Canetti, when he states: "Hitler was the crowd's own authentic leader, perhaps the first the crowd ever had" (*CM*, 286).

The question is not answered either when we turn to Canetti's analysis of the psychopathology of power, or rather it appears only in the indirect form of the irresistible attraction of power to the crowd. In the "private myth" of Schreber, this power of attraction is played out "literally" in Schreber's paranoiac delusion, that he, the last living person in the universe, is the annihilating center of attraction for vast hosts, "the totality of all souls." Schreber's "crowd in the head" offers for Canetti "a precise model of *political* power, power which feeds on the crowd and derives its substance from it" (*CP*, 512):

> Paranoia is an *illness of power* in the most literal sense of the words and exploration of this illness contains clues to the nature of power clearer and more complete than those which can be obtained in any other way. One should not allow oneself to be confused by the fact that, in a case such as Schreber's, the paranoiac never actually attained the monstrous position he hungered for. Others have *attained* it. (*CP*, 520)

Schreber's madness prefigures Hitler, but also Stalin or Mao Tse-tung, the power that feeds on the ever-growing crowds of the dead.[19] There can be no doubt that crowds have ended as the mass victims of totalitarian power. This is the justification of Canetti's separation of crowds and power. At the same time, however, it cannot be denied that crowds and power in their interaction constitute one of the most striking features of totalitarianism. What Canetti juxtaposes — the biology of the natural crowd and of power, which is only fully revealed in modernity — needs to be brought together.

On the one hand, as we have seen, crowds and power are biologically opposite in their urge to growth (increase of life, increase of death). On the other hand their biological dynamic is *politically* identical, that is to say, with each the urge to growth is totalitarian in its urge to destroy all limits. The "politics" of the crowd and power, as defined by Canetti, could therefore be summed up in terms of their common goal of the destruction of the political, the realm of instituted power (the state). In Germany, the Soviet Union, and Communist China, as opposed to Mussolini's Italy or Franco's Spain, the Party conquered the state and recognized no legitimacy outside of itself and the will of the leader. This means that while we can read with McClelland the separation of crowds and power as central to Canetti's rethinking of crowd theory, it is precisely the dynamic (biological and political) congruence of crowds and power that is central to Canetti's interpretation of totalitarianism as the natural history of modernity. What lies between crowds and power and truly separates them — the individual, the institutions of society, and so on — appears only negatively, and shrinks to nothing as it is engulfed by total mobilization and terror. It is this absence of the political, the personal and the social that makes *Crowds and Power,* and *Dialectic of Enlightenment* as well, "totalitarian" theories of totalitarianism, that is to say, deliberate provocations of their readers to force them to confront the unprecedented phenomena of our century. It is nevertheless a fundamental weakness of both works that they can offer no *political* alternative to the natural history which they so relentlessly describe. Neither Horkheimer and Adorno's reconciliation with nature nor the equality of the crowd — Canetti's version of reconciliation with nature — can substitute for political resistance to totalitarianism. Moreover, the absence of what lies between and *truly separates* the crowd and power, that is, the political sphere, points back to the crucial and central problem of the French Revolution, which foreshadows the totalitarian revolutions of the twentieth century: the reversal of the sublime instituting equality of the revolutionary crowd into the unmediated re-institution of society in the Terror, whose task is to create from above the one homogeneous body of virtue.[20] The terror that emerges from the abyss of foundation signals the failure of *political* foundation, that is, the failure to achieve the *self-limitation* of power. And when we consider the disintegration of society and its political institutions, which had been shattered by the First World War and defeat, we can see that it was precisely the naked dynamic of crowds and power that brought them together in the totalitarian revolution against the bourgeois state. The totalitarian dynamic of the crowd and of power finds its most striking expression in the idea of *permanent revolution,* whose momentum, as we shall see with Arendt, can be maintained only by permanent terror, the direct and immediate threat of death.

The Origins of Totalitarianism

Can crowd theory explain the mass support for totalitarian government? This is the question Arendt seeks to answer in relation to Hitler's and Stalin's regimes, but which is perhaps better addressed to Germany, since it is doubtful whether Stalin ever enjoyed mass support to the same extent as Hitler. In the *Origins of Totalitarianism,* crowd theory has two dimensions: the mob, by which Arendt understands the crowd, and the masses, brought into being by the industrial revolution. Mass man and mass society only emerge as a crucial political factor, however, with the disintegration of class society and class politics, set in train by the upheavals of the Great War. Although crowd theory had predicted since the early nineteenth century "the rise of the mass man and the coming of a mass age," these predictions lost much of their significance "in view of such unexpected and unpredicted phenomena as the radical loss of self-interest, the cynical or bored indifference in the face of death or other personal catastrophes" (*OT*, 316). Arendt refers at this point to Le Bon's characterization of the selfless behavior of the crowd and applies it to the psychology of mass man. In fact, as McClelland shows, Le Bon already possesses a theory of mass society, which he sees as the consequence of the political enfranchisement of the individual. Le Bon writes in *The Psychology of Socialism* (1899): "In isolating him from his caste, from his family, from social and religious groups of which he was a unit, it has left him delivered over to himself and has thus transformed society into a mass of individuals, without cohesion and ties" (*CM*, 207). For Arendt, however, the negative consequences of the enfranchisement of individuals as equal citizens appear only with the breakdown of the class system, "the only social and political stratification of the European nation-states" (*OT*, 312): "The truth is that the masses grew out of the fragments of a highly atomized society whose competitive structure and concomitant loneliness of the individual had been held in check only through membership of a class" (*OT*, 317). Arendt accordingly insists on the "decisive differences between nineteenth-century mob organizations and twentieth-century mass movements" (*OT*, 313). This decisive difference both separates and connects the crowd and the masses. The totalitarian movements were the first to realize that the "selflessness" of the crowd could be transformed into the project of "extinguishing individual identity permanently and not just for the moment of collective heroic action" (*OT*, 314).

Arendt's three key concepts are the mob, the masses (mass man), and the movement: the mob is the energizing and organizing "crowd crystal" of the masses, and together these three elements constitute the totalitarian movement. Let us look at these three ideal types, derived above all from the situation in Germany. The masses are the product of the disintegration of nineteenth-century class society, which transformed the apolitical majorities behind all parties into "one great unorganized structureless mass of furious individuals" (*OT*, 315). The psychology of these furious individuals is characterized by a sense of embittered devaluation. Self-centered bitterness, which is incapable of solidarity and can no longer identify with the "determined, limited, and obtainable goals" of class politics (*OT,* 311), goes together with a "decisive weakening of the instinct of self-preservation": "selflessness in the sense that oneself does not matter, the feeling of being expendable, was no longer the expression of individual idealism but a mass phenomenon" (*OT,* 315). Abandoned by society, the masses are ready to abandon themselves, ready to be organized and incorporated into a mass movement.[21] This is the task of the mob and its leaders, the older products of bourgeois society who precede the emergence of the masses. They, who have already broken with class society, are the *déracinés* and *déclassés,* whose activism and hatred of the system will complement the passive psychology of the masses. The revolution of nihilism thus has two components: the mob mentality of the disaffected anti-bourgeois elite (the bohemian intelligentsia), radicalized by the experience of war, and the uprooted and alienated masses. Arendt follows here what she calls the central theory of Konrad Heiden in *Der Führer: Hitler's Rise to Power:* "From the wreckage of dead classes arises the new class of intellectuals, and at the head march the most ruthless, those with the least to lose, hence the strongest: the armed bohemians, to whom war is home and civil war father-land" (*OT,* 317).

The First World War represented in equal measure a radicalizing and equalizing experience. It brought about the transvaluation of values, proclaimed by Nietzsche and embodied in the front generation of soldiers, for whom the War signified the destruction of the old world: "This generation remembered the war as the great prelude to the breakdown of classes and their transformation into masses. War . . . became the symbol for death, the great equalizer and therefore the true father of a new world order" (*OT,* 239). With Canetti we could say that this fusion of death and the crowd in war enacts the sublime moment of equality. At the same time of course, the sublime experience of the battlefield derives from the immediate experience of history as nature.[22] We can thus understand the enormous transforming force of equalization exerted by the experience of war, which gave rise to the active nihilism of the front generation, for whom destruction had become creation and self-extinction the key to renewed life. "War had been experienced as that 'mightiest of all mass actions' which obliterated individual differences so that even suffering, which traditionally had marked off individuals through unique unexchangeable destinies, could now be interpreted as 'an instrument of historical progress'" (*OT,* 329). The "self-willed immersion in the suprahuman forces of destruction," experienced in war carried over into the activism of the totalitarian movement, driven by a sense of historical inevitability (*OT,* 331).

The affinity of the intelligentsia and the mob — Heiden's "armed bohemia" — lies for Arendt in their common attraction to terroristic radicalism. The shock troops on the streets and the avant-garde's dream of cultural and political revolution are the two sides of the urge to destroy a corrupt and decadent bourgeois order. "The avant-garde did not know they were running their head not against walls but against open doors, that a unanimous success would belie their claim to be a revolutionary minority, and would prove that they were about to express a new mass spirit or the spirit of the time." And so Arendt can sum up her analysis, with its three components — the mob, the masses, the movement — in the following fashion: "It was the great opportunity of the totalitarian movements, and the reason why a temporary alliance between the intellectual elite and the mob could come about, that in an elementary and undifferentiated way their problems had become the same and foreshadowed the problems and mentality of the masses" (*OT,* 335).

In Arendt's reconstruction of the rise of fascism from the disintegration of bourgeois society, the nineteenth-century mob — as the other face of the bourgeoisie — acts as the training ground for the new type of mass leaders and agitators drawn from the *déclassé* milieu of the bohemian intelligentsia. The radicalization effected by the Great War leads to a temporary alliance between the mob and the intellectual elite; an alliance, however, in which the mob no longer functions as an agent of the elite or of the bourgeoisie (as German capitalists mistakenly thought) but solely of the masses (*OT,* 318). The mob becomes the leader of the masses and provides the momentum of the movement, whose goal is "to organize as many people as possible within its framework and to set and keep them in motion" (*OT,* 326). The decisive new dimension in Arendt's analysis is the *mass movement,* which plays no role in crowd theory. It is an ideal type, a composite drawn from the German, Italian and Soviet mobilization of the masses, which corresponds neither to Freud's artificial crowds nor to Canetti's natural or open crowd, although it shares the characteristics of each. In fact, it is *a sui generis* amalgam of both types, which in cutting across Canetti's separation of crowds and power offers a more satisfactory account of the relationship between crowds and power in totalitarianism, despite the fact that Arendt cannot make up her mind about the role of the leader. Is he a mere function or the uniting force of the movement? She writes, on the one hand, echoing Horkheimer and Adorno:

> In substance, the totalitarian leader is nothing more or less than the functionary of the masses he leads; he is not a power-hungry individual

imposing a tyrannical and arbitrary will upon his subjects. Being a mere functionary, he can be replaced at any time, and he depends just as much on the "will" of the masses he embodies as the masses depend on him. (OT, 325)

This "will" cancels the distinction between leader and led, between giving and executing orders,[23] eliminating even theoretically the difference between rulers and the ruled (OT, 325–26). On the other hand, the leader, although he is simply a function and consequence of totalitarian organization, is indispensable, and as such commands the suicidal loyalty of his entourage, since he personifies the infallibility of the movement (OT, 387). The contradiction is only apparent. In Arendt's reading of totalitarianism, the "absolute and unsurpassed concentration of power in the hands of a single man" expresses the insane will of the movement, that is to say, the "absolute primacy of the movement not only over the state, but also over the nation, the people and the positions of power held by the rulers themselves" (OT, 412). The leader is simultaneously the absolute concentration and the vacant space of power. It is this paradoxical quality which makes the leader the embodiment of the dynamic of the movement. Like the open crowd, the movement collapses once its momentum is shattered, releasing the masses, who "revert to their old status of isolated individuals" (OT, 363).

The movement possesses the qualities of both the closed and the open crowd. It shares with the closed crowd (church and army) the characteristics of organization and permanence, ideology, and fanatical loyalty. At the same time it is defined above all by the insatiable dynamic of the open crowd which recognizes no limits. After it has seized power, the movement loses neither its revolutionary momentum nor its utopian character (OT, 392), since its essence is precisely totalitarian: the inner drive for total incorporation of individuals and the outer drive for world conquest are mutually reinforcing. The unlimited momentum of the movement is thus best captured in Trotsky's paradox of "permanent revolution" (OT, 389), inseparable in practice from a permanent reign of terror. We can therefore conclude that the totalitarian movement unites in itself the autonomous, separate and opposed dynamics of Canetti's crowds and power in the form of their self-destructive fusion. Accordingly the *ultima ratio* of the totalitarian movement manifests itself in the "insane mass manufacture of corpses," preceded by the preparation of living corpses (OT, 447).

In the third edition of *The Origins of Totalitarianism* (1966), Arendt adds a final chapter, "Terror and Ideology," which draws together her theoretical conclusions regarding the unprecedented phenomenon of totalitarianism. The dynamic of crowds and power, fused in the movement, is now identified with the dynamic of natural history, whose two faces are terror and ideology. The phantasm of total domination derives its ideological justification from the claim that the movement (the Party) functions as the executive agent of the laws of nature (National Socialism) or the laws of history (Soviet Communism). The opposition between the laws of nature (Darwin) and the laws of history (Marx) is only apparent, however: "If one considers, not the actual achievement, but the basic philosophies of both men, it turns out that ultimately the movement of history and the movement of nature are one and the same" (*OT,* 463). Through the introduction of the idea of evolutionary development (perverted into the "natural" law of the survival of the fittest) Darwin showed natural life to be historical. Conversely, the Marxian driving force of history — class struggle — is based on the "metabolism with nature" through which the human species reproduces itself. The development of the forces of production rests on the natural-biological force of man's labor (*OT,* 463–64). The elevation of natural history to the law of the movement makes the essence of government itself motion (*OT,* 466), a motion without limit, which "eliminates individuals for the sake of the species, sacrifices the 'parts' for the sake of the 'whole'" (*OT,* 465). Terror functions as the executor of natural history: "Terror is lawfulness, if law is the law of the movement of some suprahuman force, Nature or History" (*OT,* 465). Its goal is to translate the imperative commands of the law into reality by accelerating the "movement of nature or history, where every single act is the execution of a death sentence which Nature or History has already pronounced" (*OT,* 467). Terror spares no one, not even its most fanatical adherents. The subjects of totalitarian rule are engulfed in a process in which "they can only be executioners or victims of its inherent law" — or both (*OT,* 468). Submission to this process is the task allotted to ideology, to the "logic of the idea," which compels submission, since it is one with the logic of the laws of movement. Ideology completes the "sublime" purpose of terror: the self-sacrificing identification with a suprahuman power.

Arendt's deduction of the essence of totalitarianism is drawn from the experience of the twentieth century. We find the very same deduction drawn with amazing prophetic insight by Georg Büchner from his study of the

French Revolution. In *Danton's Death,* which he wrote in 1834 at the age of twenty-one, Saint Just expounds his justification of the Terror in a speech to the National Assembly (for which there are no sources):

> It appears in this Assembly that there are a number of sensitive ears that cannot endure mentions of the word "blood." A number of general observations might convince them that we are no more gruesome than Nature or Time. Nature follows its laws quietly and unresistingly; Man is destroyed when he comes into conflict with them . . . I ask you now: Shall the moral universe take more consideration in its revolution than the physical universe? Shall an idea not have equal rights with the law of physics in regard to annihilating that which opposes it? Moreover, shall an event which changes the entire configuration of the moral universe, and by that I mean humanity, not be allowed the shedding of blood? The forces that move the universe make use of our arms in the world of the spirit just as in the physical world they make use of volcanoes and floods. What matter whether they die of an epidemic or of the Revolution? — The strides of humanity are slow, one can count them only in centuries; behind each one rise the graves of generations. In order to arrive at the most basic principles and discoveries, millions have had to sacrifice their lives along the way. Is it not understandable then that in an age where the pace of history is increased, all the more people should find themselves-out of breath? . . . It has required four years to make of the idea a fact; under normal circumstances it would require a century, with generations serving as punctuation marks. Is it so astounding then that the great flood of the revolution tosses up its dead at every bend and turn? . . . Humanity will rise from this caldron of blood as the earth once rose from the waters of the Deluge, with arms strong as though created anew.
>
> We herewith summon forth all the enemies of tyranny, whether in Europe or on the face of the entire earth . . . to join with us and share this [sublime] moment of triumph![24]

The two faces of natural history confront each other in the French Revolution: the sublime moment of the crowd and the sublime moment of power, each in its essence the direct expression of the instituting force of nature within history. The totalitarian movements, as conceived by Arendt, represent the attempt to give permanence to "the forces that move the universe." Terror becomes not a means but a self-propagating end in itself, which has absorbed the dynamic of crowds and power in order to annihilate the political space of freedom. If for Canetti power isolates and the crowd unites, they find their infernal fusion in the iron band of terror, which reduces each individual to helpless isolation at the same time as, by "pressing men against each other," terror destroys "the plurality of men and makes out of many the One who unfailingly will act as though he himself were part of the course of history or of nature" (*OT*, 466).

Interpreting Totalitarianism

How is the unprecedented phenomenon of totalitarianism to be interpreted? In seeking to comprehend it, our authors pose a series of conundrums. Is it the revolt against civilization in the name of race and destiny, or the dream of a self-transcending modernity that will realize the goal of history? Is it the product of the crisis and disintegration of bourgeois society or on the contrary the product of the drive to total integration? Is it the inevitable outcome of the logic of self-preservation or the consequence of the loss of the instinct of self-preservation in mass society? Is it the effect of invisible systemic apparatuses of control or the naked manifestation of the biological dynamic of crowds and power? Above all, we can ask: is totalitarianism the truth (Adorno/Horkheimer) or the negation (Arendt) of modernity? The divergent analyses of our authors do not simply reflect the complexity of the phenomenon; they are intrinsic to their very different constructions of history. Arendt's historical-political analysis, the founding classic of the genre of totalitarian studies, is far removed from the *Dialectic of Enlightenment's* critique of civilization. Canetti refuses the temptations of philosophy of history or civilizational critique by treating history as the phenomenological field of crowds and power. *Crowds and Power, Origins of Totalitarianism,* and *Dialectic of Enlightenment* are so divergent that a comparison seems at first sight willful — a conclusion that is corroborated by the absence of any such comparison in the literature on these authors. Nevertheless, my contention has been that *Crowds and Power* — a work whose neglect is the index of its hermetic nature — can best be approached by means of comparison rather than through an immanent interpretation. Canetti occupies the thematic center of the juxtaposed readings, whose guiding interest has been on the one hand, crowds and power, and, in conjunction with these, individual and mass psychology, and on the other hand, the natural history of modernity, together with excluded question of the political. In the following I briefly summarize these four lines of my comparative enquiry.

Crowds and Power

Horkheimer and Adorno construe human history as the unfolding of the one logic of domination, set in train by the self-defeating project of dominating nature, which encompasses the principle of self-preservation and the instrumentalization of reason, driven by the phantasm of total power, whose outcome is the systemic maximization of control and paranoiac destructivity. The one logic of domination thus effects a fateful and inescapable dialectic of civilization, in which totalitarian regimes represent only the most barbaric manifestation of the overall development to total integration. Canetti, in contrast, avoids the dialectical closure of history by positing crowds and power as two distinct and irreducible anthropological constants whose third term, not dealt with in detail, is society as the historical field of their undecided struggle, over which hangs the threat of the ultimate survivor and the ultimate weapon of destruction, the H-bomb (epilogue to *Crowds and Power*). Canetti's separation of crowds and power enables him, as McClelland shows, to rethink crowd theory. This theoretical gain is achieved, however, at the price of failing to confront the crucial question of the relation between crowds and power in totalitarianism, even though crowds and power, like Horkheimer and Adorno's principle of domination, share the fundamental attribute of the unlimited, that is, totalitarian urge to growth. Arendt brings the two dynamics of the crowd and of power together and fuses them in the momentum of the mass movement and the phantasmic reality of totalitarian permanent revolution. This fusion of crowds and power in the movement makes the question of the leader and his psychology dynamically irrelevant. As with Horkheimer and Adorno, the leader (whatever his personal hunger for power) is but a function of the masses and the movement. Mass psychology in this sense can be thought of as the magnification of the powerlessness of the individual projected onto the vacant space of power. It leaves no place, however, for the pathology of power, incorporated for Canetti in the paranoiac ruler, insatiable in his lust to kill. If Canetti evades the question of mass support (Arendt) for totalitarianism — the crowd in its drive "to experience for itself the strongest possible feeling of its own animal force and passion . . . will use whatever social pretexts or demands offer themselves" (*CP* 24) — both Arendt and Adorno and Horkheimer in their turn ignore the psychology of mass murder. Hitler and Stalin are not simply effects of totalitarianism.

Individual and Mass Psychology

Just as monopoly capitalism (USA) and state capitalism (Germany, the Soviet Union) replace nineteenth-century market capitalism, so mass man replaces the bourgeois individual (Horkheimer/Adorno). Comparably, for Arendt mass society replaces nineteenth-century class society. Liberal individualism no less than liberal political and social institutions fall victim to the assaults of mass movements. The submergence of the individual in the masses poses the enigma of the abandonment of the instinct of self-preservation. Although they differ in their reasons, our authors subscribe to the perception, current since Le Bon and Freud, that individual and mass psychology cannot be thought apart. Canetti shares with Horkheimer and Adorno the conviction that the reversion of the individual into the crowd or collective is inherent in the very principle of individuation, and with Arendt the conviction that the isolation of the individual in modern society, released from the older ties of religion or the newer solidarity of class, underlies the mass phenomena of the twentieth century. For Arendt the loneliness, the inability to cope with solitude, and the selflessness that comes from the experience of not belonging to the world constitute the foundation of totalitarianism (*OT*, 475). What for Arendt appears as the suicidal escape from loneliness, which drives the masses into the iron embrace of the totalitarian movement, is interpreted by Canetti as liberation from the burden of individuation and the stings of hierarchy and command. The abandonment of the self in the equality of the crowd is presented in *Crowds and Power* as the sole alternative to the deadly logic of self-preservation. What Canetti so sharply separates — the psychology of the crowd and the psychology of power, as the polar extremes of individuation — merge with Horkheimer and Adorno and Arendt into the enigmatic identity of self-preservation and self-abandonment that reduces individual psychology to mass psychology. For all of them the isolated individual has become the vacant space occupied by crowds and power, made manifest in the fantasies of individual neurosis, which repeat the great religious formations of humanity (Freud). In *Auto da Fé* individual consciousness is synonymous with blindness and the (individual) unconscious is synonymous with the crowd. The isolated individual, the atomized particle of mass society, can offer no obstacle to the totalitarian drive to domination.

The Natural History of Modernity

Whether totalitarianism is regarded as the truth or as the negation of modernity, our authors agree that it lays bare the natural history of modernity since the Enlightenment and the French Revolution, fueled by the accelerating growth of population and production, urban centers and industrial society. The dynamic of development and unlimited growth on the one hand and of unlimited control on the other is integral to western modernity. Despite Horkheimer and Adorno's intention, following Freud, of uncovering the original history of civilization, it is the history of modernity that elucidates prehistory and not the other way round. That the modern is the archaic recovers its paradoxical meaning only when we see that modernity is the original natural history, not only in the sense that it unleashes the "unnatural growth of the natural" (Arendt), that is, the elevation of the reproduction of the species to an (unlimited) end in itself, but also because modernity qua Enlightenment is itself the very origin of natural history. With the loss of the transcendent Other, which defined the heteronomy of premodern societies, nature and history emerge as the universal dynamic forces which underpin the drive for human autonomy. As Büchner had already grasped in 1834, the topoi of Enlightenment materialism — the comparison and equation of the physical and moral universe — are readily transformed into the marriage of a redemptive philosophy of history with the irresistible force of nature: "shall an idea not have equal rights with the law of physics in regard to annihilating that which opposes it?"[25] The Revolution, the very essence of modernity's acceleration of history, is itself a blind mythic force of nature; like the daughters of Pelias, it cuts humanity in pieces to make it young again. Arendt's "Terror and Ideology," in which she formulates the natural history of modernity revealed in totalitarianism, reads as an extended commentary, written by history, on the text of Büchner's Saint Just.

However, it is not only totalitarianism which threatens humanity with extinction. The "unnatural growth of the natural" has made mass society the domain of the life process,[26] which for Horkheimer and Adorno no less than for Arendt threatens to reduce man to an animal species, the slave to his "metabolism" (Marx) with nature. To these two dimensions of the natural history of modernity, crowd theory adds a third: primitive man survives in every individual, ready to return in the crowd, the collective unconscious of the individual and of society. For Freud the crowd is the oldest psychology, for Canetti the oldest animal. Its eruption threatens but also promises to return civilization to a state of nature. The "return of the repressed" can thus function as the motor of the permanent regression of civilization, ever more intensified by the "progress" of modernity (*Dialectic of Enlightenment*) or it can symbolize the recovery of an original equality that releases in the millenarian or revolutionary crowd the instituting vision of the state of nature.[27] The sublime moment of the revolutionary crowd and of revolutionary terror both involve the phantasm of an all-incorporating and irresistible force of nature, which sweeps aside all institutional limits. Behind the natural dynamic of growth — the life process, crowds, and power — there stands the ultimate datum of natural history coeval with life: the infinite debt of death, which man has always sought to placate and deflect, and which comes to unfold its full virulence with the death of God and the emancipation of the individual, who is now confronted with his own mortality. The fear of death and destruction drives the deadly logic of self-preservation: enlightenment is mythic fear radicalized. It is this fear, older and greater than the conscious self, that drives Arendt's mass man into the suicidal escape from nothingness in the totalitarian movement, the grim parody of Canetti's understanding of incorporation in the crowd as liberation from death and individuation.

The Political Realm

In his *Disenchantment of the World*, Marcel Gauchet has written a political history of religion. His thesis is simple: the history of religion is the history of the masking and alienation of the political, that is, the self-foundation of society, but also the history of the exit from religion *within* religion, which culminates in the Enlightenment. Modernity accordingly is the epoch in which society, in attaining the stage of self-institution, institutes the political realm. But, as we know, the French Revolution — the paradigm of the new foundation — also brings forth from the political the terroristic practice and ideology of totalitarianism. Totalitarianism's liquidation of the political makes it the negation of modernity and its highest value — self-limiting freedom. At the same time, it can also be comprehended as the negative truth of modernity, that is to say, as the return of the repressed, which re-institutes in the name of necessity or destiny the absolute heteronomy of society. However, it is precisely because Horkheimer and Adorno comprehend totalitarianism as the return of the repressed, that is, as the natural history of modernity, that they possess no concept of the political. This deficit is the fatal legacy of Marxism's dismissal of politics, human rights, and morality as the "bourgeois" façade of capitalist domination. The result is a totalizing construction of modernity that is itself totalitarian in its liquidation of plurality and difference. In the dark night of domination the difference between limited and un-limited power, the political and the totalitarian, becomes minimal. Ca-netti's natural history of modernity likewise brackets the political. The political realm, as that which alone separates and mediates between crowds and power, remains a vacant space, invaded and occupied by the expansive dynamic of crowds and power. The free association of individuals appears with Canetti only in terms of its other — the crowd — and plays no role in *Dialectic of Enlightenment*. The individual alternative to domi-nation that Horkheimer and Adorno and Canetti offer takes the form of a reversed mirror image of natural history — with Canetti it is the capacity for transformation by means of which the individual (and the artist) liberates himself from the petrifying prison of self-identity and regains contact with the mythical realm of metamorphosis; with Horkheimer and Adorno it is the capacity for mimesis by means of which the indi-vidual (and the artist) recovers the "remembrance of nature in the sub-ject" (*DE,* 40). Only Arendt possesses a theory of the political,[28] which is already present in *The Origins of Totalitarianism* and is de-veloped in her subsequent work. It is her defense of modernity in the face of the horrors of the twentieth century, the horror that is so directly present in Horkheimer and Adorno's and Canetti's provocation of the reader.

3: Religion, Crowds, and Power

THE MYTHS AND RELIGIONS of mankind are a constant subject of reflection in Elias Canetti's *Aufzeichnungen*, which cover a period of fifty years from 1942 to 1993. Although the pervasive presence of myths and religions in *Crowds and Power* has been frequently noted and has begun to attract closer attention, it cannot be said that the relationship between religion, crowds and power has been adequately studied.[1] Here it would seem that Canetti is to blame in his insistence that the nature of the crowd and of power can be grasped only in and of itself. Crowds and power are presented as primary data: the irreducible but at the same time the reductive anthropological source of history as the eternal return of the same, driven by the endless cycle of self-preservation and extermination, culminating in the mass wars, the genocidal regimes of the twentieth century and the ultimate weapon of annihilation. In such a view of history, culture is reduced in the last instance to nature, for are not death and the fear of death the ultimate instance that inhabit and impel crowds and power? Axel Honneth exemplifies this perception when he defines Canetti's image of man and society as the perpetuation of the archaic state of nature.[2]

But if death is the ultimate biological datum, the greatest of natural evils (Hobbes), it is by the same token the primary source of humanization, of culture and religion. It is Ernst Cassirer who reminds us that attributing the derivation of myth and religion to fear fails to recognize that what is most essential in the religious life of man is not the *fact* of fear but the *metamorphosis* of fear.[3] In other words, the history of mankind can be neither articulated nor interpreted outside of the universal process of the cultural transformation of "the state of nature." My contention is that we should not take the natural history of crowds and power as the genetic key to human history. I believe that we cannot understand crowds and power apart from religion and that we cannot understand the history of crowds and power separately from religious history from the earliest myths to the world religions; only such a reading is capable of giving a more adequate account of the tension between nature and culture in human history that occupied Canetti throughout his life. In *Crowds and Power* Canetti writes: "It is not possible to give an exhaustive interpretation of religions here; that will be the subject of a separate work" (*CP*, 150). This separate work, like the promised continuation of *Crowds and Power,* has not appeared. In what sense, however, could it be a separate work? Religion, crowds, and power belong together, and it is the dynamics of their relationship and of the interplay between them that must be explored.

This will be the focus of the second and third parts of the chapter, in which I compare Canetti's religious history of crowds and power with Marcel Gauchet's political history of religion in *The Disenchantment of the World,* with a side glance at Cassirer's *The Myth of the State.* In the first section I shall return briefly to the genesis of Canetti's conception of the crowd in the 1920s, with reference to *Auto da Fé.* In the last section I shall consider Canetti's religion in the light of the irresolvable tension between nature and culture in his thought, the tension, in Weber's words, between empirical reality and the conception of the world as a meaningful totality, which religious teachings and then philosophy have sought to resolve.[4]

The Crowd Experience

Canetti's account of his fascination and possession by the phenomenon of the crowd in the second part of his autobiography, *Die Fackel im Ohr* (1980, The Torch in my Ear) has all the qualities of a religious awakening. It begins with the overwhelming *experience* of the mysterious and seductive power of the crowd. It is followed by the overwhelming moment of *illumination,* in which the meaning of the crowd experience is revealed in a sudden fierce sensation of expansion: the *revelation* that there is a crowd drive in opposition to the personality drive and that from their strife the course of human history can be explained. From this original illumination, Canetti drew the strength to devote thirty-five years of his life to the search for an explanation of what the crowd really is and how power arises from the crowd and reacts back on it.[5] At the beginning stands the physical experience of the crowd, the knowledge of the crowd from within, the sense of charismatic possession that separates Canetti from all scientific studies of the crowd. It is his conviction that description and analysis without experience represent a false path. The fatal distinction between subject and object cuts us off from the vital truth of experience. This is the essence of his rejection of Freud's *Group Psychology and Ego Analysis* (1919): Freud and the authorities on which he draws, chiefly Le Bon, are closed to the crowd. They treat it as an alien and frightening phenomenon, a kind of illness, whose symptoms must be described.[6]

The opposition between illumination and blindness, living intuition and rational dissection, which announces the themes of *Auto da Fé*, needs to be seen in the intellectual context of the 1920s. The critique of modern civilization in the novel stands in the tradition of *Lebensphilosophie* since Schopenhauer and Nietzsche. The original title of the novel — "Kant fängt Feuer" (Kant catches fire) — signaled the conflagration of reason, the suicide of the head without world, of the blind intellect which has separated from and turned against life. The topoi of *Lebensphilosophie*: intellect against life, head against world, and living and dead culture are driven here to the apocalyptic limit, in order to reveal life, the world, the crowd as the limit of rationality and the illusions of individuation. Let me just stress the epistemological consequence, which informs Canetti's thought not only here but throughout his life: the conviction that cognition is rooted in intuition, in the holistic and mimetic grasp of phenomena prior to all philosophical categories and scientific classifications and that only such intuition can give us access to the world.

There is, however, another formulation of the distinction between living intuition and rational analysis, which comes from the sociology of religion, and is equally pertinent to our theme. Max Weber's distinction between prophets and priests can be applied to the antithesis embodied in the brothers George and Peter Kien in *Auto da Fé*. The psychiatrist George is reborn through his moment of illumination, which leads him to turn his back on conventional science and proclaim the truth of the crowd as the origin and goal of human history, the coming redemption from the sufferings of the *principium individuationis*. Like his author, George prides himself on one discovery alone: "and it was precisely this: the effects of the mass on history in general and on the life of individuals" (*AF*, 462). For all the irony that permeates the novel and which by no means excludes the prophet, we can observe here the imaginative projection of Canetti's own sense of personal calling, which distinguishes the prophet from the priest, who lays claim to authority by virtue of his service to a sacred tradition. To the priest corresponds the scholar Peter Kien, dedicated to the sacred tradition of learning, blind to the chaotic reality outside and inside the walls of his library, or George's professional assistants and colleagues in the mental asylum, whose routinized indifference to the charisma of their mad patients calls forth his scorn: "Those few among us who have faith still cling to experiences which were lived for them by others thousands of years ago. We need visions, revelations, voices — lightening proximities to things and men — and when we cannot find them in ourselves we fetch them out of tradition. We have to have faith because of our poverty. Others, still poorer, renounce even that. But look at him! He is Allah, prophet and Moslem in one. Is a miracle any the less a miracle because we have labelled it *Paranoia chronica*?" (*AF*, 455).

Canetti, George, the madman: prophets mirrored in the prophet. According to Ernst Fischer, Canetti himself, like his figure George, believed at the time in a coming redemption through the crowd, spreading irresistibly out from Asia.[7] But what was this distant millenarian prospect compared to the Thousand Year Reich in the heart of Europe? The prophet withdrew into the wilderness of exile and silence. Intuition had to school and discipline itself in the exhaustive study of human history and cultures if it was to be equal to the challenge of the century: the totalitarian symbiosis of crowds and power. *Auto da Fé* was the prophetic diagnosis of the apocalypse of civilization and at the same time the germ of *Crowds and Power*, which would appear thirty years later. In his autobiography Canetti writes that the significance of the crowd in religions had begun to dawn on him in the 1920s and that it was the origin of his desire to know all the religions of the world.[8] For George, as we have seen, the poverty of our times comes from the loss of a living faith, the decline, in Spengler's terms, of culture into civilization. Of the religion of the past there remain only the "private myths" of the isolated individuals in *Auto da Fé*. For Freud, who dismissed the oceanic feeling of religious sentiment as an infantile illusion, they represent the individual neuroses of post-religious society; for Canetti they are precisely the neuroses of the individual, delirious testimonies to the separation of modern man from the crowd. In George's words: "sometimes the masses pour over us, one single flood, one ocean, in which each drop is alive, and each drop wants the same thing. But it soon scatters again, and leaves us once more to ourselves, poor solitary devils" (*AF*, 461).

A Political History of Religion

Thirty years of silence separate *Crowds and Power* from *Auto da Fé*: thirty years of immersion in the study of history and with it a growing distance from the charisma of the crowd. In the mid-1950s Canetti notes, "As regards the crowd itself, I have lost my earlier prejudices, it is for me neither good nor bad but *there,* and the blindness towards it in which we have lived up to now is intolerable to me" (*NH*, 12). This does not lessen either the enigma or the historical significance of the crowd as something distinct from power. The *and* of *Crowds and Power* separates rather than couples, and represents for J. S. McClelland Canetti's distinctive contribution to the political theory of the crowd since Plato, which brings this whole tradition to a conclusion. McClelland is undoubtedly right in reading Canetti in the context of political theory, since it is clear that the totalitarian conception of politics is central to the whole investigation. It is also clear, however, that the question of modern politics is tied up with the larger perspective of religious history, and that this larger perspective is crucial to gaining the cognitive distance that alone will enable Canetti to "seize this century by the throat" (*PM*, 234). As he writes: "A 'modern' person has nothing to add to modernity because he has nothing to set against it" (*GU*, 97). Canetti's opposition to modernity, indeed to history, involves a fundamental reversal of historical perspective. Against the history of the historians and their celebration of the religion of power he turns to the precious record of mankind's myths and religions (*NH*, 204) but with the knowledge of the frightful exhaustion of the gods (*PM*, 141).[9] This reversal of perspectives, captured in the statement: "We come from too much, we are moving towards too little" (*PM*, 83), looks to the past to rescue the future and is directed in equal measure to comprehending and escaping from the blind logic of growth and power. We, not our ancestors, are the true barbarians (*PM*, 146). The modern, progressive conception of history has blinded us to the original cultural creativity of the primitives, which constitutes for Canetti an unchangeable and living revelation, but also the temptation to escape from the present and disappear into an overwhelming origin (*PM*, 197–98). Canetti's fundamental opposition to evolutionary history makes prehistory the measure of history, a reversal that in turn is the measure of his will to rethink everything from the beginning, to think outside of the functional categories of the human and social sciences in order to recover the enigma of human history, the riddle of the crowd, of power, of the social bond, of religion and faith, which he calls the central and greatest riddle of his life (*PM*, 110).

We find a comparable sense of enigma and a comparable reversal in Gauchet's political history of religions. Gauchet's highly original argument, which takes up the legacy of Emile Durkheim, Mircea Eliade, and Pierre Clastres, is, I think, particularly helpful to a deeper understanding of *Crowds and Power,* since it helps to bring into focus what remains implicit in Canetti's phenomenological approach, above all the tripartite division of history they have in common: the all-important break between prehistory and history, and within history the emergence of the modernity that inaugurates post-religious society.

Like Canetti, Gauchet distances himself from the dead hand of historicism and scientism in order to rethink human history from its beginnings:

"The study of 'non-literate' people provided the main challenge to the naive evolutionist model of history driven by growth." ". . . hidden in the depths of time is another humanity, whose secret has been lost, and needs to be rediscovered." (*DW*, 87) What is this secret that challenges our comfortable notions of civilization? Gauchet argues that the essence of religion must be sought in its natural, supposedly elementary forms, where it occupied the whole social space and provided the key to the social bond. Seen in this light, the subsequent history of religion represents not an advance but a retreat, a retreat marked by the rise of politics, set in train by the emergence of the state around 3000 B.C., which divides history into two: on the one side societies *prior* to the state, on the other institutionalized domination. The rise of the state is thus the crucial event in human history and the first religious revolution: "This is where our five thousand years of 'history-as-growth' really began, a period that was ridiculously brief and amazingly swift compared to the unimaginably long *durée* from which they arose. After dozens of millennia with religion dominating politics, followed by five millennia with politics dominating religion, we are at the point where religion has been systematically exhausted" (*DW*, 9).

Everything in Gauchet's political history of religion rests on his anti-evolutionary and anti-materialist interpretation of primal religion. Societies prior to the state are not societies without a state but societies *against* the state, a formulation that Gauchet takes over from the anthropologist Pierre Clastres. They are societies which refuse politics, that is, society's active control over itself through a separated power. This refusal must be grasped not as incapacity but as an unconscious collective decision embodied in primal religion, which anchored human inscription in the natural world and the equality of the social group in the absolute anteriority of its ordering principles. Human self-possession depended on radical self-dispossession in relation to the pre-given foundation and its cosmic order stemming from the immemorial time of origin, repeated and renewed in myth and ritual. This absolute self-dispossession, which allowed only the sovereignty of tradition and in refusing politics enabled humans to live in cultural harmony with nature over thousands of years, constitutes for Gauchet the deepest enigma of human history. If this history without growth represents the outcome of unconscious choice, this unconscious choice was nevertheless free, since it cannot be reduced to external determination (*DW*, 29).

It would seem that the self-dispossession of humans, given by the temporal anteriority of the Other, is as nothing compared with the political and religious dispossession effected by the growth of state power. On the one hand, given that "power continually strives to increase itself" (*DW*, 41), slavery is the logical consequence of despotism. On the other hand, the despot needs new personal deities, powerful enough to legitimate the imperial thrust of domination. Hierarchy is instituted as the unifying difference of society, which replicates at every level the relation of society to its foundation, represented by divine kingship. This first religious revolution had, however, a double consequence. If the rise of the state signified the destruction of the original equality of the social bond and a breach in the unity of the cosmos, the religious universalism called forth by imperial universalism — the axial religions of the first millennium B.C. — opened up an interior fracture in being that gave access to a higher truth and order of reality beyond communal existence and the human and cosmic hierarchical chain. Gauchet distinguishes here between the two new types of order: the immanent impersonality of underlying identity in China and India, as opposed to transcendent subjectivism in the Middle East and the birth of rationality in Greece. The dynamic of religious transcendence opens up a political dialectic in the West that Gauchet formulates as follows: the greater the gods, the freer humans became. The entire significance of religious history for Gauchet is revealed and comprehended in this "law of human emancipation through divine affirmation" (*DW*, 51). In short: the idea of the omnipotent creator god, which replaces and reverses the immemorial order of primal religion, makes the unfolding conception of an intelligible deity the index of the development of human reason. The idea of the sovereign god and his sovereign representative in the world thus leads finally to a conception of sovereign power distinct from religion. The simultaneous development of the absolutist state and of modern individualist theories of the social contract in the seventeenth century indicates the correlation between the sovereign state and self-constituting society: "The democratic inversion of sovereignty was from its very beginning inscribed in sovereignty understood as the idea of the modern state, as the expression of the new relation between power and society resulting from the completed revolution in transcendence" (*DW*, 58). This revolution is an achievement unique to western history and as such the outcome of a history which is religious to the core. Christianity is thus to be understood as the religion of the exit from religion. Gauchet relates the story of the original self-dispossession of humans, overthrown by the advent of the state and of history-as-growth, in the course of which political and religious dispossession leads finally to human self-possession beyond religion. It is a story with a happy democratic end, based on the categorical distinction, hidden in a footnote, between democracy and totalitarianism, that is, the argument, reserved for a future book, which rejects "the idea of an omnipresent structural possibility of totalitarianism within contemporary societies" (*DW*, 219).

It is here of course, in their reading of modernity, in which politics takes the place of religion, that Gauchet and Canetti part company. More important for our purposes, however, is that they start from a common premise, a common conception of religion as *religio*, as the essence of the social bond, that is to say, the reciprocity of the social and the religious, which is most fully realized in the moments of mass excitement which unite the group. The classic sociological account of religious excitement as the expression of the collective and anonymous force of the social group is to be found in Durkheim's analysis of totemic religion among Australian Aborigines in *The Elementary Forms of Religious Life*. Durkheim speaks of a state of general effervescence which he sees as recurring throughout history in revolutionary or creative epochs, evident for instance in "many of the scenes, either sublime or savage, of the French Revolution."[10] For Durkheim, as for Canetti, the elementary forms of religious life provide the source of the great ideas and the principal ritual practices of even the most advanced religions.[11] But unlike Durkheim (who is conspicuously absent from *Crowds and Power*) Canetti confronts the reader with the elementary forms as such of the crowd, the pack, the elements of power, the command, transformation, and so on, as discrete phenomena drawn from the most diverse times and places, apparently without "any sense of historical differentiation."[12] It is here that Gauchet can help us to come to terms with Canetti's attempt to escape from the historical observation of the world, to gain a vantage point *outside of history*, outside of the five millennia of history-as-growth, and the corresponding methodological estrangement of progressive and evolutionary conceptions of history, expressed in the determination to think from the beginning (*PM*, 159). That is, Gauchet can help us to articulate the historical relation between crowds and power, between the religious and the political, and between nature and culture, and thus to disengage the underlying historical conception of *Crowds and Power*.

A Religious History of Politics

We must begin with the crucial distinction between prehistory and history, between societies before and against the state and the institutionalized domination of hierarchically stratified societies. The original unity and solidarity of human groups appears for Canetti most clearly in the pack, in which the social bond finds its concentrated collective expression. Here the equality of the group means that the social and the religious are one. Their non-differentiation is rooted in the oldest law of justice, the regulation of distribution (*CP*, 211). The concrete unity of action of the pack contains the origins of mass behavior, just as the distinct forms of the pack — for hunting, war, lament and increase — and their transmutations have become the substance and core of every important faith (*CP*, 110, 150). The pack thus represents the prehistory of crowds and religions but not of *state power*. Since the equality of the group precludes the emergence of a separate political power, we cannot look to archaic society for explanatory clues to modern politics. On the contrary, it is the exit from prehistory, from the socioreligious unity and equality of human groups, that lays the foundation for the rise of the state and the enslavement of humans, and stands at the beginning of the accumulation and growth of power: "Once men had succeeded in collecting large numbers of slaves, as they collected animals in their herds, the foundations of the tyranny of the state were laid" (*CP*, 445). This is why Canetti is careful not to conflate crowds and power, since the crowd for him always recalls and enacts the original unity and equality of the social group, and why we must distinguish between the prehistorical world of myth, which primarily involves the cultural mediation of *nature,* and the historical epoch of the axial universal religions, where the cultural mediation of *power* assumes primary importance. We can discern a reflection of this historical break in Canetti's fundamental ambivalence towards the religions of transcendence — Judaism, Christianity and Islam — which is nowhere evident in what he calls his hunger for myths.

One can perhaps best summarize the significance of myths for Canetti under two headings: the original cultural creativity of prehistory and the stark contrast he sets up between this mythical creativity and history. In 1971 he writes: "That one will never again escape history is for me the most devastating thought. Is it the real reason why I occupy myself with all myths? Is it in the hope of a forgotten myth which could rescue us from history?" (*NH*, 190). In a similar fashion, he proposes archaeology as the key to our future in the past: "An unexpected discovery could alter our own, still undetermined (*unbestimmtes*) fate" (*PM*, 202). Like Gauchet, he feels himself a pygmy in relation to the treasures of prehistory. He laments his poverty and the shallowness of modern knowledge compared with that of an Arunda elder, but he knows that the elders are dead, that their myths and traditions exist only in books, in the books that are his sacred texts (*NH*, 18). If for Canetti the essence of man lies in transformation and play (*PM*, 92), this essence is most fully revealed in the mythical imagination of the long *durée* of prehistory, against which he registers the progressive creative and spiritual impoverishment of history. Did we, he asks, exhaust our creative possibilities in the old myths (*PM,* 102).

It is a question addressed to the world religions of the axial breakthrough in the wake of the establishment of imperial states. Let me preface my comments on the relation between religion and politics with two reflections of Canetti on the relation between monotheistic religion and polytheistic myth: "So much has been lost with the gods of the ancients that one could fear that something will be lost with our own, simpler God. But I cannot find my way back to him, who brought death into the world" (*PM,* 340). "Is not [this love for the names of the old gods] penance for the one God, whom the ancestors imposed on the world, the impoverishment and desolation [*Verödung*] which they conjured up with him?" (*NH,* 174) In these reflections we observe the theme of the One and the Many, the question with which philosophy begins in the thinking of the pre-Socratics, to which Canetti feels particularly close, in contrast to his hostility to the subsumption of the Many under the One in the onto-theological tradition of Western philosophy and religion. Canetti distinguishes between the occidental and oriental axial religions in terms of their disenchantment of the world, that is, their relation to the Many, the natural cosmic order from which they emerged and in terms of their relation to power. If prehistory signifies the overwhelming origin and source of cultural creativity, China represents everything that Canetti associates with civilization: that is, with the civilizing effects of culture on power.[13] Canetti's observations on Chinese civilization occur in the central chapter (the sixth of eleven) of *Crowds and Power,* "The Survivor," where the Chinese cult of the ancestors is credited with having realized a mutually rewarding link between the generations that defuses the resentment of the dead and the secret triumph of the living: "Piety towards the dead and awareness of the self have entered into alliance. [. . .] If one reflects on the figure of the ideal ruler as it takes shape in Chinese history and thought one is struck by its humanity. It is probable that the absence of brutality in this image is due to the particular form of ancestor worship" (*CP,* 317).

Although Chinese civilization is presented as an ideal alternative to Western civilization, not least because Confucianism and Taoism — "the religion of poets" (*PM,* 325) — did not break with the ancestral traditions of cosmic order, it is to occidental monotheism that Canetti turns to exemplify the rise of world religions from the dynamics of packs, e.g. Christianity as a religion of lament and Islam as a religion of war[14] and in its Shiite branch as a religion of lament. The religion of increase becomes by contrast a world religion only in modernity in the form of the complementary visions of production (capitalism) and distribution (socialism). In the chapter entitled "The Pack and Religion" the basic distinction between myth and religion and between the pack and the crowd is subordinated to the historical distinction drawn between this chapter and the following, "The Crowd in History." History here refers not to the historical development inaugurated by the advent of the state but to the period of modern nation states. The historical epoch of the world religions is related to its prehistory and in the case of Christianity distinguished from its post-history, the transformation of religion into politics in the modern era. From the perspective of either a political history of religion or conversely a religious history of crowds and power, the political revolution effected by the modern transition to post-religious society in Europe is of course central, and I will therefore focus on what Canetti sees as its determining feature: the eruption of the *open* crowd out of the disintegration of the *closed* crowds of Christianity. We can thus postulate for the three stages of history an underlying correlation between the pack and myth, between the closed crowd and axial religion, and between the open crowd and the political dynamic of crowds and power. The distinction between the pack and the crowd corresponds to the distinction between prehistory and history but also implies a history of transformations between myth and religion. The distinction between the closed and the open crowd corresponds to the break between religious and post-religious society but also to a history of secularizing transformations between religion and politics.

For Canetti the *natural* crowd is the open crowd with its urge for unlimited growth. Its most conspicuous quality — destructiveness — can be regarded as the manifestation of its iconoclastic fury ("The destruction of representational images is the destruction of a hierarchy which is no longer recognized" [*CP*, 20]), which gives expression to the primal desire for equality that turns the instituting force of the social against instituted society. This urge to unrestricted growth, which makes the open crowd the enemy of all hierarchy and institutionalized domination, also defines the aims, dynamic and appeal of universal religions in their early stages. Over time, however, "institutions which offer solidarity and permanence seem more and more important to them" (*CP*, 26) and the task becomes the domestication of the crowd of the faithful, their subordination to the institution, with its rites and ceremonies, through the substitution of repetition for growth, the fiction of equality for real equality, and distant salvation for immediate goals. In sacrificing growth the closed crowd gains permanence. It has become a slow crowd, the crowd in a state of fasting, which is held together by the remoteness of its goal, whether it be the Promised Land for the Israelites, the pilgrimage to Mecca for Mohammadans, or the invisible goal beyond this world for Christians. And it is only when faith in the other world begins to decay that the slow crowd of Christianity starts to disintegrate (*CP*, 47).

Canetti devotes a section to the Catholic Church's unparalleled mastery over the crowd: "There has never been a state on earth capable of defending itself in so many ways against the crowd" (*CP*, 182). This mastery represents the outstanding example of the triumph of instituted religion over the original instituting faith, and this means that it has for Canetti a historical significance and a historical legacy different from those that Gauchet attributes to Christianity as the religion of the departure from religion. The historical significance of the Catholic Church, underlined by its development of an elaborate administrative hierarchy, resides in its ability to control and channel religious enthusiasm; that is, to tame the natural crowd. The open crowd only becomes historically important when it "has freed itself from the substance of traditional religion" (*CP*, 23). Canetti therefore proposes a close link between such eruptions and secularization, which can be related in turn to the comparison he draws between the closed religious and the open political forms of reversal crowds. Whereas the revolutionary crowd is driven by the urge to immediate deliverance from the burden of the stings of command that have been implanted by long submission to domination, the closed crowd contents itself with the future reversal promised by religion ("The last shall be first"), which calls for present submission to divine commands (*CP*, 66–71). The historical significance of Catholicism relates not only to the containment of the crowd but also to its continuation of the inheritance of the Roman Empire. The triumph of instituted over instituting religion, in Canetti's words, of Christendom over Christianity, signified the victory of Rome. Twenty Christian centuries served to clothe and preserve the Roman idea of imperial conquest, which has re-emerged in its old and naked form in the twentieth century (*PM*, 42–43). Accordingly, Canetti distinguishes between the secular legacy of Christianity — the centuries of belief in Christ's divinity have endowed the suffering and dying son of man with a kind of earthly immortality that has given a new earthly value to the individual (*CP*, 543–44) — and the secular legacy of Christendom: the eruption of crowds and power in their modern, naked form, freed from "the substance of traditional religion."

In other words, it is only when the restraining hold of traditional culture over crowds and power finally disintegrates that the *nature* of crowds and power is fully revealed. It is necessary to insist on this point in order to reverse the conventional readings of *Crowds and Power* and to clarify the difficult question of the relation between nature and culture in Canetti's thought (which I will take up again in the last section). This reversal can be formulated in terms of the paradox: the (idea of the) state of nature stands not at the beginning of human history but at the beginning of modernity. At the beginning of human history we find not nature but social groups with comprehensive cultural interpretations of being-in-the-world, in which the political is completely subsumed in the religious. These societies against the state are prior to crowds and power and to the separation of society and power in the state. The imperialism of the state and the concomitant emergence of universal religions unfold the manifold and complex interplay between culture and power. Gauchet characterizes this period as the epoch of the political domination of religion, and Canetti examines it from the perspective of the religious domination of crowds but also of the mobilization of the faithful as in the Crusades or in the Holy Wars of Islam. This epoch is succeeded in the West by the emergence of modern, post-religious society, where for Gauchet the whole democratic tendency to reunify society and power has become the horizon of modern politics (*DW*, 174), whereas for Canetti of course the unleashed dynamic of crowds and state power constitutes the central challenge to historical understanding.

The paradox that the state of nature stands at the beginning of modernity is to be understood in a double sense. The one, *overt* sense is given in the statement in *Crowds and Power* that it is only in modernity, due to the enormous increase of population, the rapid growth of cities, and the liberation from the substance of traditional religion, that we can see the crowd "in its nakedness, in what one might call its biological state" (*CP*, 23). In other words, the natural history of crowds and power begins with modernity. Roberto Calasso speaks of "naked society" as the consequence of society's incorporation of the religious in the course of the nineteenth century: "What was left in the end was naked society, but invested now with all the powers inherited, or rather burgled from religion. The twentieth century would see its triumph. . . . The power and impact of totalitarian regimes cannot be explained unless we accept that the very notion of society has appropriated an unprecedented power, one previously the preserve of religion."[15] The second, *covert* sense in which we can speak of the state of nature at the beginning of modernity concerns the early modern theories of the social contract and Canetti's concealed debate with political theory. The significance of Hobbes for modern political theory lies in his break with religious thought and his determination to think from the beginning by posing the question of political power in terms of the "natural condition of mankind," that is, mankind's "perpetual and restless desire of Power after power."[16] *Crowds and Power* stands within this Hobbesian tradition of radical inquiry, which it pushes to the limit by questioning Hobbes' absolute distinction between nature and culture, natural and civil history, that follows from the act of the self-foundation of society against the state of nature. If Canetti speaks of destroying Hobbes' conception of power (*PM*, 170), it is because he cannot accept Hobbes' distinction between the will to power in nature and in the state. In protecting us from nature, the voluntary and unconditional submission to the sovereign power of the Leviathan perpetuates the state of nature. The roots of power and the tyranny of the state spring from the fear of death. Conversely the essence of the parliamentary system lies in the renunciation of death as an instrument of decision (*CP*, 222).

Gauchet also sees Hobbes as a key figure in his political history of religion; not, however, in the light of his anthropological image of man as *homo homini lupus* (man is a wolf to man), but in the light of the liberal and democratic reception of Hobbes's severing of the concept of sovereignty from its religious legitimation. According to Canetti, as we have seen, the disintegration of the containing power of religion confronts us with the naked forms of crowds and power. Nevertheless, it remains the case that this natural history of modern politics is grasped and articulated in religious categories in *Crowds and Power*. Thus the chapter "The Crowd in History" begins with the religion of nations as expressed in their national crowd symbols. These symbols are the modern successors to the invisible crowds of all religions since animism. Gauchet likewise speaks of the nation as the invisible terrestrial being arising from the social body (*DW*, 186). Of these invisible crowds Canetti observes: "They are the lifeblood of faith. . . . When they fade, faith weakens and, whilst it dies slowly away, fresh hosts come to take the place of the faded" (*CP*, 52). This slow process of fading and secularizing transformation and renewal can be contrasted with the rapid form of secularization brought about by the sudden prohibition of a faith, which Canetti illustrates with reference to the army, the crowd symbol of the united German nation after the Franco-Prussian war of 1870–71. August 1914, when the German people became an open crowd, was the moment of the conception of National Socialism. The Treaty of Versailles, which disbanded the German army, was the moment of its birth: "The prohibition of the army was like the prohibition of a religion." "Every closed crowd which is dissolved by force transforms itself into an open crowd to which it imparts all its own characteristics. The party came to the rescue of the army, and the party had no limits set to its recruitment from within the nation" (both *CP*, 212).

Canetti returns to the central question of National Socialism in the final chapter of *Crowds and Power*, "Rulers and Paranoiacs," in which he justifies the detailed exposition and analysis of Schreber's *Memoirs* by the insights they offer into the nature of power and by the far-reaching coincidence to be discerned between Schreber's paranoiac system and the ideological system of National Socialism. Again, it is striking that Canetti turns here to a "self-created religion" (*CP*, 505), that is, to a private myth comparable to those that populate his novel and testify to the secularization of the lost collective religion in the eruption of mad fantasies of crowds and power in the individual. The study of "The Case of Schreber" is a direct continuation of *Auto da Fé*. Moreover, it is here that Canetti addresses the question of the relation between politics and religion. He defends his political interpretation — the thesis that Schreber's delusions provide "a precise model of *political* power, power which feeds on the crowd and derives its substance from it" (*CP*, 512) — against the objection that these apocalyptic visions are inherently religious by insisting that "religion and politics are inextricably intermingled": "The Saviour of the World and the Ruler of the world are one and the same person. At the core of all is the lust for power" (*CP*, 520).

Not only does the conclusion of *Crowds and Power* point back to *Auto da Fé*, but the conclusion of Gauchet's *Disenchantment of the World* also places us before Canetti's vision of the human condition in his novel, the condition in which we are "destined to live openly and in the anguish from which the gods had spared us since the beginning of the human venture." To live, that is, "the mercilessly contradictory desire inherent in the very reality of being a subject." "Perhaps we will never find a true balance between self-love that wishes to exclude all else and the desire to abolish the self, between absolute being and being-as-nothingness" (both *DW*, 207). In this polarity of absolute being and being-as-nothingness we recognize Canetti's original polarity between the personality drive and the crowd drive, from which he will derive the primal phenomena of power and the crowd.

Canetti's Religion

> *Nothing can save us that is possible:*
> *We who must die demand a miracle*
> — W. H. Auden

In arguing that *Crowds and Power* needs to be read as a religious history of politics, I have intended a double revision. First, to call into question Canetti's supposed ahistorical naturalism by reversing the relation between nature and culture. Second, to explain and exemplify this reversal by reference to his anti-evolutionary reading of human history as a process of spiritual impoverishment leading from culture to natural history, from the original mythical creativity of societies prior to and against the state to the naked forms of crowds and power in modernity. Precisely Canetti's unremitting hostility to history and the religions of state power excludes the appeal to the archaic and the "primitive" to explain such modern political phenomena as National Socialism. In this respect he stands at the opposite pole to Cassirer's enlightenment conception of history, which views National Socialism as the return of myth. And here it is significant that Cassirer turns to the first founding myth of the *state*, the Babylonian epic of creation, in order to demonstrate that the world of culture "could not arise until the darkness of myth was fought and overcome."[17] Against this enlightenment figure of the return of the repressed, Canetti states that National Socialism grew out of "formations and tendencies of an entirely unprecedented kind . . . which are only now beginning slowly to be understood" (*CP*, 210). In other words, we are dealing here with events that call for historical understanding. Further, the whole question of nature and culture in *Crowds and Power* can only be understood historically. Canetti's naturalism stands, as we have seen, in the tradition of Hobbes's radical inquiry, whose precondition was the collapse of the religious legitimation of the social bond and social order in the religious wars of the sixteenth and seventeenth centuries. If there is a developmental logic in Western history, it is for Canetti one overshadowed by the exhaustion of the gods. "Of the Beyond," he writes, "there remains only Nothingness, its most dangerous legacy" (*PM*, 163). The knowledge of the transience of the world religions compared to what preceded them, the knowledge that no religion is indestructible, the knowledge that the death of the Christian God has made death our mortal god, this is the historical key not only to Canetti's naturalism but also to Canetti's religion. In 1976 he states: "I have not allowed myself to have a god. . . . I wanted to find out how one endures [*besteht*] alone" (*GU*, 52).

Canetti's religion and naturalism belong together[18] because it is only with the disintegration of the substance of traditional religion that human history and human being become an irreducible and irresolvable enigma. Only after the retreat of religious culture does the question of nature and culture impose itself as the radical question, to be pushed to its unsettling and disturbing limit in *Crowds and Power*. Only after the death of the Beyond, the death of immortality, does the impossible question of religion emerge as such. Canetti's religion — the refusal of death and its power over us — is the secularized inheritor of the world religions of lament (cf. the epilogue to *Crowds and Power*). Deprived of the promise of resurrection, it asserts itself as the impossible religion, for were it not impossible it would not be a religion, would not be an absolute and universal religion *against nature*.[19] It is evident that this religion after religion, directed against the illusion of salvation in the hereafter, is compelled to confront the blindness of nature, to seek for the roots of crowds and power in the greatest of natural evils. It is also evident that such a radical confrontation can allow itself no way out. He notes in 1975: "You could escape only in another attitude to death. You can never escape" (*GU*, 39).

We are thus confronted with the paradox that Canetti's absolute *religious* refusal of nature drives him into the despairing acknowledgment of *naturalistic* closure, which haunts his thought throughout and returns undiminished in his final "Aufzeichnungen." "Everything, that ever served for killing, every word, every view, every conviction returns. That is the *only* Eternal Return." "How senseless all this refusal [*Abwehr*] now! If only it looked different out there! But it seems to be worse and worse. What is it that one wants to rescue? Devilish human nature that grows ever more devilish?" (*AZ*, 40, 76) And his last reflection on *Crowds and Power:* "The one who wanted to come to grips with power and wrote the textbook (*Lehrbuch*) of power" (*AZ*, 93). And yet this despairing sense of failure is directed just as much against the reader as against himself. It dictates the whole strategy of *Crowds and Power:* "The form of *Crowds and Power* will become its strength. With the continuation you would have destroyed this book by your hopes. As it is now, you compel the readers to seek *their* hopes" (*GU*, 161).

What Canetti sees as characterizing myth — its combination of constancy and inner fluidity (*PM*, 24) — can be applied to his own thought. It is structured from the beginning by the tension and interplay between the personality drive and the crowd drive, that is, between closure and openness, the One and the Many, and this tension in turn characterizes his religion. The one pole is defined by the *one* question of death and power and its refusal, which lock nature and anti-nature in an inescapable circle, a closure, which constantly seeks its other pole. Canetti's horror of systems would not be so great if he did not recognize in himself the compulsion of the prophet to reduce the Many to the One by confronting us with the one inescapable question. The ambiguity of this tension is particularly evident in a notice from the late 1950s: "Do the myths contain *everything*, as I often like to tell myself, or is there something else beyond all myths? — Is there a new myth, one completely unheard of, and am I here in order to seek it? Or will I end pitifully and miserably with a mere inventory of all myths?" (*NH*, 19). One myth or all myths, the one, new myth of the prophet or all the myths of the priest, the custodian of the sacred texts? These opposed tendencies, embodied in the brothers George and Peter Kien, belong together in Canetti's religion: the call of prophecy that draws him close to the two radical thinkers of early modernity, Hobbes and Pascal — "Only Pascal knew everything" (*AZ*, 89) — and the duty of *piety*, which he so much admires and respects in the Chinese. The desire to know and live in all the myths, the desire to know all religions as though one believed in them (*PM*, 93), is integral to Canetti's religion. This lifelong immersion in the religious legacy of human history is his form of ancestor worship, dedicated to the resurrection of dead and forgotten cultures and their gods: "What have I ever done but demand the restitution of the immortality of the gods" (*AZ*, 43).

What then is Canetti's image of man? Is man the wolf who perpetuates the state of nature (Honneth) or is man the symbolic animal (Cassirer)? The epilogue to *Crowds and Power* presents our split future, poised between closure and continuation since the atom bomb: "Today either everyone will survive or no one" (*CP*, 546). For the sake of survival, Canetti confronts us with the closure of history. We could say that the tendency to harness the Many to the One predominates in *Crowds and Power* and that the equally vital counter tendency, the repository of Canetti's hopes, is held back. In this sense the (absent) continuation of *Crowds and Power* is closely linked with the continuation of human history. Precisely in connection with the nuclear destruction of Hiroshima he states: "There is no end for the creative thoughts of humans. In this curse lies the only hope" (*PM*, 92). And in the following entry he speaks of transformation and play as constituting the essence of man. It can hardly be doubted that *transformation* would have been central to the continuation of *Crowds and Power* and to the separate book on religions, since he attributes the very possibility of human culture to transformation:

"Everything that a man can do, everything that represents his culture, he first incorporated into himself by means of transformation" (*CP*, 254). This fundamental cultural capacity carries within itself, however, in comparable fashion to Adorno's concept of mimesis, its shadow: the will to transform animate and inanimate nature into objects of domination and incorporation, which has only unfolded its full potential in the modern epoch. Such deadly mimesis, such "identity thinking" with its prohibitions on spontaneous transformation, forms the very antithesis to the opening to and enrichment of our relation to the world. The positive capacity to identify with others, and with the Other, goes hand in hand with the self-transformative capacity of humans (see chapter 4). And at the heart of this self-transforming creativity we must place the mythical transformations of nature as the basis for the religious transformations of power. The atrophy of cultural creativity is, as we have seen, one of Canetti's recurrent charges against modernity. He points to the modern separation of faith and production and correlates the absence of new stories with the mass production of new things (*PM*, 305). We lack, in other words, a new myth, a new religion, that would be capable of defusing and civilizing the dynamic of growth and power: "Knowledge will only lose its deadliness through a new religion, which does not acknowledge death" (*PM*, 63). Again, he writes: "Transformation would depend on being overwhelmed by new gods, in which you believe" (*GU*, 134).

Transformation is, we may conclude, the crucial missing link, the withheld key to Canetti's thinking on culture. He warns himself against treating it as a universal panacea, but he also speaks of having left the key unturned in the lock (*PM*, 47, 241). Whatever the reasons for this reticence, the consequence is clear: the central role of the imagination and symbolic expression in human creativity, the understanding of cultures as "imaginary significations" (Castoriadis) has not been examined. Behind the great caesuras of human history, which separate history from prehistory and political society from religious society, lies the immemorial divide between nature and culture. This is why, as I have sought to demonstrate, Canetti's radical inquiry into the nature of crowds and power can only be articulated as a religious history stretching from the collective religious creativity of the pack and its inner transformations to the self-created religion of Schreber on the threshold of the twentieth century.

4: Canetti's Counter-Image of Society

> *It could be conceivable that society is not*
> *an organism, that it has no structure, that it*
> *functions only temporarily or seemingly. The*
> *most obvious analogies are not the best.*
> — The Human Province

> *True, he [man] wants to "preserve"*
> *himself, but he also simultaneously wants*
> *other things which are inseparable from this.*
> — Crowds and Power

> *The planning nature of man is a very*
> *late addition that violates his essential, his*
> *transforming nature.*
> — The Secret Heart of the Clock

> *Man, regarding himself as the measure*
> *of all things, is almost unknown. His progress*
> *in self-knowledge is minimal, every new theory*
> *obscures more of him than it illuminates.*
> — The Conscience of Words

THE STRANGE CASE of Canetti's *Crowds and Power* — widely recognized as a key work of a major writer, but virtually ignored as a contribution to social theory — can only be explained in the context of a more general discursive blockage. There is no denying that Canetti's image of man and society is an exceptionally hermetic and idiosyncratic one, but it is in some ways comparable to other deviations from the mainstream.

The idea of a pluralistic or "multi-paradigmatic" character of modern social thought is misleading in that it obscures the underlying strength of unquestioned — and often inarticulate — notions that constitute the common ground of otherwise different interpretations, affect the understanding of historical experience, and obstruct the formulation of fundamental alternatives. Some contemporary authors have subjected these background assumptions to extensive criticism and argued that social theory should be reconstructed in explicit opposition to them; details will not be discussed here, but the objections to the dominant image of society seem to center on three main points. It is *over-integrated,* in the sense that the emphasis on unity grounded in shared meaning (conceptualized as norms and values or — in a more critical vein — as pervasive ideology) obscures other aspects of social life; *over-rationalized,* inasmuch as the components or subsystems of the social whole are supposed to obey an overall design; and *over-subjectivized,* because society is more or less explicitly cast in the role of a collective actor or a macro-subject.[1] In the present context, the effect of these presuppositions on our understanding of power is of particular importance. The impact of power on social life is circumscribed, streamlined and sanitized: power becomes, in other words, an instrument: a medium or a resource under the control or jurisdiction of more fundamental forces. This inadequate conception of power is, as various critics have argued, the most visible shortcoming of mainstream sociological theory, but also a key to its unacknowledged origins. The dominant image of society is — according to this now well-known view — an idealized image of the nation-state, and it serves to transfigure the role that power plays in the creation and maintenance of the latter.

One of the less debated questions raised in the wake of these criticisms has to do with the history and legacy of alternative traditions. There are countercurrents within the mainstream of modern social theory; there are also — more important for our present purposes — separate lines of thought that stand in stark contrast to the dominant image of society and draw on experiences which it failed to account for. Crowd or mass psychology is an obvious case of the latter kind. The following discussion of its core ideas and its challenge to social theory is largely based on Serge Moscovici's reconstruction of its history.[2] But if crowd psychology can be understood as a marginal counter-project to the main body of the sociological tradition (and a useful corrective to shortcomings of the latter), Canetti's work is in turn related in a similar way to crowd psychology. We are thus dealing with a deviation from a deviation, an outsider's heterodox response to a half-established heterodoxy. This double estrangement makes it difficult to bring Canetti's ideas into discursive contact with more conventional views.[3]

Mass Psychology and Its Legacy

If we want to use Moscovici's reinterpretation of mass psychology as a bridge between these different universes of discourse, a few words should first be said about its particular bias. Moscovici is aware of Canetti's work, but does not make much use of it; there is nevertheless a fundamental affinity between the two authors in that they are interested in the pathological tendencies of power, their relationship to crowd formations, and their manifestations in recent history. But their ways of posing and exploring these problems have little in common. Moscovici opts for a critical dialogue with the key figures of mass psychology and confronts their ideas with twentieth-century historical experience in order to develop their insights beyond their explicit formulations. His approach reflects the disillusionment that has set in among those who once took a more optimistic view of crowds as collective actors: "At the beginning of the century we were certain that the masses would triumph, whereas towards the end of it we are all the prisoners of leaders. One after another, the social upheavals that have shaken most countries in the world have brought to power a regime headed by a charismatic leader."[4] The focus is, in other words, on totalitarian outcomes of transformative projects, and the regimes in question — together with related phenomena, such as wars, revolutions, and radical mass movements — are the historical realities most obviously out of line with the dominant image of society. It is true that Moscovici was writing at a time when totalitarian states were much stronger and seemed more viable than they do at the end of the century. But the global failure of the Soviet model should not be mistaken for a final answer to the question of totalitarianism.

Mass psychology as a tradition — and a quasi-discipline — developed in response to troubling by-products of the modernizing process. More precisely, it explores things neglected by Marxist thought as well as by the sociological alternatives to Marxism, and it does so — from the outset — with a keen awareness of vast but ambiguous political implications. "Collectives . . . made and unmade by the breakdown of social ties, the speed of communications, the continual mixing and fusion of populations and the accelerated and exhausting pace of urban life," and then "reconstituted in the form of unstable and ever-greater crowds"[5] are highly visible on the modern social scene; the decisive reason for taking mass psychology seriously is that its account of such phenomena has yet to be absorbed by the theorists of social systems or conflicts. But a critical reading of its seminal texts has to confront the preconceptions that obscured their message. Gustave Le Bon, widely acclaimed as the founding father of mass psychology (and however questionable the originality of his work may be, he was undoubtedly the most influential pioneer), saw crowds as a potential threat to order and civilization.[6] His analyses of the mental life and behavioral patterns of crowds were therefore meant to serve a political purpose: the aim was to develop techniques of control and leadership that would help to ensure the survival of a conservative version of liberal rule in the conditions of mass society. In view of his unequivocal commitment to the powers that be, Moscovici's reference to him as the "Machiavelli of mass societies" seems inappropriate. Le Bon's view of the fin-de-siècle situation — his most widely read work was published in 1895 — was much less detached than Machiavelli's survey of the world of early monarchies and declining city-states. It is true that some contemporaries tried to give a more critical twist to Le Bon's ideas; for example, Georges Sorel suggested that the reality and the idea of the class struggle could change the character of crowds and make them more capable of genuinely radical action. Under such circumstances, the insights of mass psychology might be adaptable to the agenda of a revolutionary movement with proper understanding of collective beliefs and myths as instruments of mobilization. But there is no doubt that the main reason for widespread interest in Le Bon's writings was their overt political appeal.

However, it is one thing to restore Le Bon to his rightful place in the history of ideas and another to take a theoretical interest in his work. Moscovici justifies the latter approach by claiming (to my mind convincingly) that Le Bon pushed his line of argument to a level that can be fully grasped only in retrospect and in relation to similarly neglected ideas in classical social theory. The most decisive step was to generalize the notion of the crowd beyond conventional views. Prior to Le Bon, crowd phenomena had been seen as more or less aggressively deviant, but in any case secondary, by-products of a society built on more solid foundations. In discarding these preconceptions, Le Bon discovers — at least in principle — that "the mass is the basis of society, . . . the raw material of all political institutions, the potential energy of all social movements and the original state of all civilisations."[7] This basic fact has become more visible in modern societies and has created new problems — but also new opportunities — for those who strive to maintain order and authority without traditional foundations. The new understanding of masses or crowds as a universal — but more particularly modern — substratum of sociocultural patterns is reminiscent of Durkheim's search for a more elementary and creative state of social life beyond normative structures. But Le Bon differs from Durkheim — as well as from authors of other less conclusive attempts within the sociological tradition — in that he sees the pre-structured state as utterly devoid of autonomy and creativity. The masses may be a necessary and omnipresent raw material for social construction; this does not alter the equally basic fact that the constructive effort and vision must come from elites, and a failure of the latter would lead to chaos rather than to any creation from below. In the end, Le Bon's broadening of the scope of crowd psychology thus serves to justify more sweeping claims on behalf of leaders and authorities. But the rethinking undertaken for this purpose had opened up possibilities of further reflection on crowds as a key to social life. This fundamental ambiguity of Le Bon's approach is more obvious to late twentieth-century readers than it was to his contemporaries.

For Moscovici, one of the merits of mass psychology is that it calls into question the strict separation of sociological and psychological perspectives, which was proclaimed as a first principle by the founders of sociology and still widely taken for granted. Moscovici's own critique of this dogma is inspired by his desire to enhance the status and expand the boundaries of psychology.[8] Doubts about the division are likely to be raised by any major effort to rethink the framework of social theory, but it is by no means self-evident that they should lead to an upgrading of psychology. Some other options will be discussed below. At this point, however, it is more useful to consider the implications of mass psychology for the dominant image of society.

As noted above, mainstream sociological theory was overly concerned with and overconfident of integration. Not only was there a strong emphasis on the specific integrative aspects of social life; above and beyond that, the theorists in question try to construct a model that brings integration into an orderly balance with other basic functions and determinants. Division, differentiation, and rationalization thus appear as essentially coordinated with the prevalence and progress of integrative mechanisms. We might describe this vision of the social world, most forcefully defended by Parsons, as an integration of integrative and non-integrative features. And it is precisely this higher-order primacy of integration that is — at least implicitly — called into question by mass psychology. A one-sided but insightful account of the real forces making for unity in social life upsets the idealized picture of order in progress. If the core idea of mass psychology was that the fusion of individuals into a crowd entails intellectual regression, a strengthening of the unconscious at the expense of rationality and reflection, and an irresistible homogenization of mental life, the theoretical implications are obvious: this phenomenon represents a simultaneous intensification and impoverishment of the social bond. We are, in other words, dealing with a paradoxical form of social integration, self-absolutizing in its radically de-differentiating drive, but at the same time its regressive impact on the social constructions of individuality, rationality and autonomy undermines the very preconditions of integration. Alongside this theoretically deviant but practically dominant version of integration, mass psychology analyzes a particularly radical form of social division: the separation of leaders and elites from the masses. In so doing, it reveals — as Moscovici shows — some of the pathological potential of power in modern society that was later exemplified by totalitarian rulers. But this critical reading goes beyond the intentions of the founders. Their aim was, rather, to explain and justify the monopolization of power as a counterweight to the growing strength of the masses. The characteristics that make masses dangerous to civilization are, in the last instance, identical with those that make them dependent on leaders; it is a matter of turning the latter effect against the former.

In short, the insights of mass psychology disrupt the dominant image of society and suggest the possibility that the structures that seem to validate it might be superimposed on a less orderly and less easily definable level of social life. That is, as we shall see, a theme which Canetti was to develop in a more original and disconcerting fashion. But first we must briefly consider Freud's transformation of mass psychology; a critical response to this project was the starting-point of Canetti's work, and Moscovici's reinterpretation of Freud may help to understand what is at stake in Canetti's search for an alternative to psychoanalytical approaches.

Freud wanted to put the study of crowd behavior and mentality on a more solid psychological footing than the pioneers had been able to do, and for him this could only mean a psychoanalytical grounding; since Le Bon and others had already underlined the regressive role of the unconscious in crowd thinking, the connection with Freud's own more elaborate theory was easily established. Similarly, Freud's definition of the discipline echoes and extends the generalizing turn taken by Le Bon: "Mass psychology thus treats the individual human being as a member of a tribe, a people, a caste, an estate, an institution or as a part of a human aggregate that organizes itself as a mass for a certain time and for a certain purpose."[9] In view of these logical steps beyond an incomplete legacy, Moscovici describes Freud as Le Bon's "best disciple." But the psychoanalytical version of mass psychology — together with some related texts — can also be seen as a significant extension of Freud's own project; Moscovici uses a somewhat daring comparison with Einstein's move from restricted to general relativity to underline this point. The analogy has at least the merit of highlighting the speculative character of the "general psychoanalytical theory" that grows out of the encounter with mass psychology. It poses the problem of power and authority in relation to the evolving mental life of humanity, whereas restricted psychoanalysis was only concerned with the transformations of the individual psyche within the family context. In presenting the more general and speculative theory as Freud's major achievement, Moscovici is of course departing from all psychoanalytical orthodoxies of letter or spirit; his aim is to develop a more adequate account of twentieth-century power of leaders over masses on the basis of Freud's ideas.

Freud focuses on two particularly important types of "artificial," that is, organized masses: church and army. This does not mean that he is oblivious to the more chaotic crowd formations that had been so disturbing to the founders of mass psychology. But he takes for granted that large-scale organizational patterns with strong authority figures are superimposed on more elementary levels of collective life. The advantage of singling out the two key institutions is that they exemplify the essential connection between masses and leaders and allow us to understand it in a way that also throws light on the whole complex of social constraints. For Freud, it is the dynamic of identification — a derivative but distinctive form of the libidinous drive — that explains the attachment to leaders as well as the more diffuse commitment to social and cultural ideals of various kinds. Moscovici reconsiders this argument in the light of historical experience and revises the metapsychological assumptions: a reconceptualization of mass psychology should start with the duality of *eros* and *mimesis,* that is, "two groups of desires, those of inamoration, whose function is to turn the individual away from himself and unite him to others, and the mimetic desires representing a propensity for identity and exclusive attachment to another person, a specific model."[10] This new frame of reference makes it possible to improve on Freud's analysis in two crucial respects. On the one hand, the recognition of mimetic desires as independent, polymorphous and adaptable enables Moscovici to do more justice to their historical transformations, and in particular to the extreme turn they have taken in the secular religions and totalitarian systems of the recent past. The complex processes of identification on which they are based include reactivations of archaic models of authority; the "return of the repressed" can thus be seen from a more historical perspective than it was in Freud's myth of the primal horde. On the other hand, the distinction between *eros* and *mimesis* allows us to view ambiguity and tension as inherent in the relationship between leaders and masses.

The mimetic patterns of authority block or absorb other tendencies of masses in formation: "mimesis finishes what Eros starts."[11] But this also means that we can envisage a radical response that would draw on the insights of mass psychology to maximize the democratic potential of modern societies. Moscovici ends with speculation about post-liberal democracy, unprecedented in the whole tradition that he proposes to reconstruct.

Situating Canetti

This retrospective upgrading of mass psychology will help us to appreciate its theoretical reach and thus to grasp the significance of Canetti's challenge to it. But for an adequate comparison to be possible, we must first note some obstacles inherent in Canetti's work. One of the most obvious is the fragmentary character of his *magnum opus*. The planned second volume of *Crowds and Power* was never written; although the same thing has happened to other ambitious works, the problems created in Canetti's case are as unique as his project. The text of *Crowds and Power* does not follow the conventional course of theory-building. Rather, Canetti foregrounds and elaborates the ideas most provocatively at odds with established images of man and society, so as to maximize the isolation of his own intellectual world. This strategy is, moreover, unevenly applied and only in part effective: some key themes of the books — as we shall see — are strikingly less developed than others. We can therefore assume that the second volume would have filled the gaps in the first and then gone on to present a more complete alternative to the mainstream. But on its own, the first volume is too incomplete to bear comparison with more systematic — albeit thematically related — works such as *Dialectic of Enlightenment* or *Origins of Totalitarianism*.

More important, Canetti's way of constructing and using concepts poses interpretive problems of a very peculiar kind. As he once put it, he cared so little for concepts that at the age of fifty-four, he still had not properly read Aristotle and Hegel (*NH,* 24). This should not be taken too literally: there is no doubt that the typology of crowds and packs as well as the analysis of power and survival are based on a distinctive set of concepts. But the features and functions of these concepts need further clarification. His disregard for received rules of concept formation goes so far that it may sometimes seem more appropriate to speak of theory-laden images. To begin with a crucial point, the polemic thrust of Canetti's constructs, acknowledged in principle, is mostly left unstated on the level of particulars. Key notions derive much of their meaning from opposition to more orthodox views, but Canetti does not spell out the details of this constitutive antagonism. The result is an artificial and deceptive isolation of conceptual building-blocks, further aggravated by the paucity of explicit connections within Canetti's own frame of reference. And this lack of integration is, in turn, not unrelated to the uncertain contours of each category. Canetti tries to keep his concepts flexible and porous enough to reflect the widest possible range of human phenomena; this approach is reminiscent of his description of Stendhal, one of his few acknowledged models, whom he praises for never "trying to construct spurious unities" (*CP,* 323).

A third problem has to do with Canetti's extensive use of anthropological sources. There are no historical, cultural, or disciplinary limits to his inquiry into the human condition, but primitive societies and religions are obviously his favorite keys to more general insights. This preference for the primitive world can lead to misunderstandings of his aims. He has been accused of relying on an obsolete evolutionist anthropology; if we define evolutionism in a theoretically relevant way, that is, in terms of assumptions about general developmental trends in history (and not simply as the search for archaic origins, which can take very different forms), the criticism is clearly unfounded. A more plausible interpretation suggests that Canetti wants to unmask civilization as a "perpetuation of the state of nature."[12] The reconstruction of archaic antecedents and determinants in various areas of human life is indeed one of the main concerns of *Crowds and Power,* but this line of thought is pursued in a very peculiar fashion, and we should not impute to Canetti the theoretical premises inherent in arguments about the state of nature and its persistence behind the façade of civilization. The very notion of a state of nature only makes sense in contradistinction to another state that must in some way — irrespective of otherwise different definitions — be seen as transcending nature. In early modern thought, this idea was linked to some version of social contract theory, but more recent variations on the same theme are — roughly speaking — based on historicism: their cornerstone is, in other words, the idea of history as a movement beyond nature or that of culture as an order against nature. Even those who want to argue that the state of nature prevails over such alternatives need a weakened or self-relativizing notion of its opposite to make their point. For example, the negative philosophy of history developed by Adorno and Horkheimer ("human history . . . continues the unconscious history of nature, of devouring and being devoured")[13] uses a truncated version of Marxist theory to describe the progress that in the end serves only to perpetuate and reactivate the most elementary relations between humanity and nature. No background assumptions of that kind enter into Canetti's project. But his perspective is equally — even if less obviously — incompatible with the culturalist one. In fact, he rejects the very concept of culture, and his main reason for that is closely related to a central theme of his whole work. The idea of culture is, as he sees it, inseparable from the fictitious reconciliation with death that has been a common aim of dominant religious and philosophical traditions; Canetti regarded his own effort "to enhance the consciousness of death" (*GU,* 159) as unique among philosophers. An early aphorism puts it forcefully: "The purest expression of culture is an Egyptian tomb, where everything lies about futilely, utensils, adornments, food, pictures, sculpture, prayers, and yet the dead man is not alive" (*PM,* 36).

Some further aspects of Canetti's anti-culturalist stance will be discussed below; as we shall see, it does not prevent him from developing ideas which can be read as contributions to cultural theory. At this point, however, we should note its implications for the use of anthropology. The conceptual distinction between culture and nature is central to the modern anthropological project from the nineteenth-century founders to Lévi-Strauss and the various offshoots of his legacy; interest in the cultural constitution of primitive societies has been accompanied by the persistent but adaptable idea that they are in some sense closer to a natural condition, and the interplay of these two themes has given rise to both relativistic and universalistic theories. (For present purposes, we can disregard the conventional labels of social and cultural anthropology; they refer to branches of a shared tradition.) Canetti's relationship to anthropology is perhaps best described as an attempt to bypass this whole universe of discourse while retaining access to the experiential field on which it is based. For him the primitive world is a vast collection of clues to the human condition, but if we want to use them properly, we must first neutralize the interpretive schemes that have hitherto done more to blunt than to enlighten our empathy. This generalized skepticism goes beyond specific theories, and questions the whole self-understanding of anthropology as a discipline: when Canetti says that he prefers to read about primitives, rather than meeting them face to face, he is obviously expressing doubts about the orthodox conception of fieldwork as essential to the understanding of primitive cultures and societies. A detailed assessment of the results of this approach cannot be attempted here, but the intention is clear and is closely related to other aspects of Canetti's work. It is, more specifically, in line with the last quotation at the beginning of this chapter: the self-knowledge of man is still very limited and the first precondition for further progress is detachment from its established frameworks.

Finally, it may be suggested that Canetti is not as completely isolated from main currents of twentieth-century thought and therefore not as inaccessible to comparative reading as his own statements can lead us to believe. In particular, his affinities with phenomenology have hardly been noticed. It is now well established that echoes and variations of the phenomenological turn in philosophical thought go far beyond the phenomenological tradition in the narrow sense.[14] When Canetti speaks of "the avoidance of the concrete" as one of the "most sinister phenomena in intellectual history" and attributes it to a human "tendency to go first after the remote things" (*GW,* 25), rather than paying attention to the elementary levels of experience, he is striking a phenomenological chord: his way of turning "to the things themselves" may lack the conceptual refinement of the better-known versions, but some parallels can nevertheless be drawn. The detailed description of concrete and familiar but neglected or misrepresented phenomena, central to the analysis of both crowds and power, may be seen as Canetti's access to the lifeworld. The emphasis on bodily aspects and determinants of human conduct is reminiscent of themes that came to the fore in phenomenological thought after its turn against transcendental idealism. And although Canetti's studious avoidance of any reference to Heidegger is no doubt motivated by the sense of a diametrically opposite attitude to death, in both cases the return to concrete experience and manifest essentials of the human condition reactivates the question of death, even if the answers are incompatible.[15]

The Crowd as Vision and Experience

We must now turn to a closer analysis of Canetti's encounter with mass psychology and — less directly — with the intellectual background to this new discipline. The crucial step, decisive for everything that follows, is his reinterpretation of the crowd phenomenon.[16] According to his own testimony, this was done in response to Freud's psychoanalytical version of mass psychology. In a late interview, Canetti refers to *Group Psychology and Ego Analysis* as a futile exercise that failed to come to grips with real crowds.[17] He would not have accepted the excuse that the analysis of church and army could take for granted the work of earlier mass psychologists on more elementary forms of collective life. For Canetti, this was to put the cart before the horse: mass psychology had not grasped the constitutive characteristics of the phenomena that it proposed to study, and a radical shift of perspective was needed to rectify its errors. His autobiography contains a brief account of the birth of this idea from experience as well as from a critical reading of

Freud. Two encounters with real and active crowds (significantly, both events — in Frankfurt 1922 and Vienna 1927 — were workers' demonstrations) convinced him of the importance of the forces at work in such cases, and of the need to know them better. Between these encounters, an inner experience that Canetti describes as an "illumination" deepened his understanding of what was at stake; but it was his confrontation with Freudian theory that led to his first efforts to construct a new frame of reference. Although Canetti insisted on the original and fundamental character of the crowd experience, which he saw as no less elementary than hunger or libido, his approach to it was at first more similar to Freud's than it became during the work on *Crowds and Power*. He experimented with the notion of a "mass drive" opposed to either the libido or a less Freudian "personality drive"; no such metapsychological dichotomies are used in his mature work.[18]

Canetti's account of his relationship with Freud is clear and convincing. But the same cannot be said about the treatment of another author whose work is at least as crucial as Freud's to the understanding of *Crowds and Power*. Canetti makes no mention of the chapter on aboriginal ceremonies in Durkheim's *Elementary Forms of the Religious Life* (surely the most important analysis of a crowd scene in classical sociology), but it is impossible to believe that he did not know it. He may have attributed the religious activity described by Durkheim to packs rather than crowds (he saw totemic rituals as typical of the "increase pack," which will be discussed below), but the point is that Durkheim's account of "collective effervescence" raises questions and develops ideas intrinsically related to those involved in Canetti's crowd theory. Religious ceremonies bring the dispersed fragments of aboriginal societies together in a temporary but intensive union that makes the individual "think and act differently than in normal times" and feel "as though he really were transported into a special world, entirely different from the one where he ordinarily lives, and into an environment filled with exceptionally intense forces that take hold of him and metamorphose him."[19] This higher level of collective life explains the genesis and periodic renewal of religious ideas, and the crowd as a creative force thus becomes the fountainhead of human civilization: all institutions of moral and material life are, in Durkheim's view, derived from religious origins. The analysis of elementary patterns is only a first step towards the understanding of more complex and controversial developments. (The aboriginal ceremonial gathering is for Durkheim a recognizable ancestor of the revolutionary crowd.) Durkheim admits that the contrast between routine and creative states may not be as clear-cut among civilized peoples, and the particular role of crowd formations therefore not as obvious, but then his argument leads to a question that he never tackled in a systematic fashion, and which has not been highlighted by later interpretations and adaptations of his work: in what ways and to what extent is the archaic pattern of collective effervescence transfigured into other forms of social self-creation?

We can now analyze Canetti's conception of the crowd in relation to the two very different paradigms represented by Freud and Durkheim. There are three key aspects that set his project apart and are best understood as responses to their perceived shortcomings.

First, the impact of the crowd on the individual — more precisely: on the social constitution of the individual — is analyzed in a more balanced and comprehensive way. For the founders of mass psychology, the mental life of crowds was regressive in that it gave free rein to unconscious processes and archaic patterns; Freud accepted this thesis as a basic insight, linked it to his own theories, and went beyond it only inasmuch as he tried to show that individual regression could be conducive to institutional progress: the task of "artificial groups" was to re-establish on a collective (and therefore enlarged) scale the control, organization and authority that were essential to the mature individual. Durkheim's notion of collective effervescence is, by contrast, meant to highlight the enriching, creative and empowering effects of crowd formation (at least in the privileged cases that fully reveal its potential). Institutions (beginning with the meta-institution of religion) emerge out of this collective crucible and therefore cannot be explained as projections of individual goals or guidelines. Canetti describes the fusion of individuals in a crowd as a *transformation* that negates a whole preexisting order and opens up a new field of possibilities; in itself and in general terms, this radical change is neither regressive nor uplifting, although such terms may be more or less applicable to specific results. It is, in other words, one-sided and misleading to speak of an abdication of individual autonomy or an escape from atomization and routine; the crowd experience is, more fundamentally, a move from one social world to another. Hierarchies, divisions, and distances are characteristic of a self-perpetuating social order; by contrast, the crowd takes shape when "distinctions are thrown off and all feel *equal* . . . when no one is greater or better than another . . ." (*CP*, 19). The conventional social framework of individuality is abolished, but the real significance of union in a crowd for the individuals involved depends on the context.

Second, the mechanism of the transformation is located at the most elementary level of experience. Canetti abstains from speculation about the mental states and mutations that had been a prime concern of the psychology of crowds. Instead, he gives a phenomenological account of the state of consciousness involved in the formation of crowds: it is the "reversal of the fear of being touched," the release from the constant effort "to avoid physical contact with anything strange" and the "feeling of relief" in surrendering to the crowd (*CP*, 16). The implications of this reversal cut across boundaries between domains of mind and life. Both the fear of being touched and its reversal represent a fusion of perception and emotion. More important, they seem to be described in terms that allow for extension beyond the social realm: the shift from fear of the unknown to the feeling of "everything . . . happening in one and the same body" (*CP*, 16) affects the whole relationship of the human being to the world. This blurring of the distinction between the social and the non-social makes it easier to understand how crowd images can be projected onto other levels of reality and natural phenomena perceived as symbolic counterparts to crowds. Here we may feel reminded of Durkheim's analysis of the interpretive connections between society and its environment (social structures are transfigured into cosmic patterns, and natural objects are incorporated into the self-representation of society), but Canetti tries to tackle the question at a less speculative and more intuitively accessible level.

Finally, the two social worlds mentioned above are interrelated but not reducible to common rules. For Freud and Durkheim, there is a unitary and unambiguous core structure of social reality. Freud's "artificial groups" are presented as more perfect embodiments of the principles that are already at work in ephemeral crowds, whereas Durkheim's effervescent crowd brings the individuals into more direct contact with their own social essence and thus reveals the underlying truth of their everyday life. Canetti's crowd is more akin to a counter-society: its dynamic is at odds with established structures, and its intermittent presence makes a more explicit contestation possible. "All demands for justice and all theories of equality ultimately derive their energy from the actual experience of equality familiar to anyone who has been part of a crowd" (*CP*, 32). For Canetti, the crowd — more precisely the "true crowd" (*CP*, 21), that is, the open, uncontrolled and unconstrained one — is thus the experiential basis of imagined alternatives to the social order. The momentary meltdown of institutions in the expanding crowd serves to bring out the difference between established and possible institutional patterns. But such visions of another social world can only be understood as products of an imagination that takes off from the crowd experience. On this point, Canetti's analysis leaves something to be desired. In a discussion with Adorno, shortly after the publication of *Crowds and Power*, the question is raised in a revealingly inadequate way. In line with his own emphasis on the primacy of the object, Adorno accuses Canetti of one-sided concern with the subjective side of crowd phenomena. Canetti's response is oddly defensive and inconclusive: he insists on the material reality of his main objects of inquiry and avoids the question of their subjective dimension. A closer reading of his work suggests that a very distinctive view of the latter — of the crowd imaginary, to use a concept derived from Castoriadis — is essential to the argument even if it is often dressed up in deceptively objectivist language.

The role of the creative imagination is most obvious in the case of the "invisible crowds" (from the dead to angels, devils and bacilli) that figure prominently in mythical religious and scientific world-views. An imaginary element is also involved in the construction of "double crowds" on the basis of binary distinctions; visions of the living and the dead, men and women, or warring parties as opposed to and at the same time constitutive of each other go beyond concrete crowd experiences. Less obvious but more fundamental are the imaginary aspects of the dynamic that Canetti regards as a common denominator of crowd phenomena. The four basic traits or defining characteristics of the crowd as such — the drive for growth without natural boundaries, the imperative of absolute equality, the maximization of density, and the need for movements towards a goal (*CP*, 32) — are not objectively given and cannot be described from the perspective of an external observer. Rather, they must be understood as imaginary projections of perceptions from within; in ascribing drives or dispositions to the crowd, Canetti is spelling out the logic of a collective phantasm that transcends all observable states and disregards inherent limits to its aspirations. He may talk about the crowd in its most elementary form as if it were a quasi-biological phenomenon, but this is a case of methodological self-misunderstanding (not without some similarity to Freud's scientist misrepresentation of his half-theorized discovery of the imagination).

Canetti's interpretation of the crowd is set out in apparent isolation from the broader context of social theory, but its implications cannot be fully appreciated without reference to other perspectives. The vision of untroubled unity, unconditional equality and unanimous collective action, derived from the inbuilt self-image of the crowd, invites comparison with the above-mentioned dominant image of society. Seen against this background, Canetti's crowd appears as a rather paradoxical pattern of social life: a perfect society that dispenses with any specific articulations or mediations of the social bond, and hence transcends the tensions inherent in all historical forms of integration. The crowd strives for integration without the ambiguous (enabling and limiting) effects of institutions; it aspires to act in com-mon without any separate coordinating instances; and its pursuit of a goal reveals an elementary but unmistakable rationality. Those who denounced the chaotic, destructive and irrational character of crowds failed to grasp these more fundamental features and made too much of the "disintegration of the crowd *within* the crowd" (*CP*, 29). In brief, Canetti's account of the crowd can be read as an emphatic but at the same time indeterminate version of ideas that recur in more complex and qualified forms within the main-stream of social thought. Even the radical egalitarianism of the crowd, its most obviously subversive attribute, is not wholly alien to orthodox socio-logical theory. From Durkheim to Parsons, the notion of "institutionalized individualism" serves to graft a limited but persistent equalizing logic onto the dominant image of society. The result is the well-known conception of citizenship as a gradually evolving expression of a normative order. The point of Canetti's *aperçu* about justice and equality is that crowd experiences are crucial to the ideals and innovations that are then reinterpreted as or-ganic products of social development. It seems likely that a sequel to *Crowds and Power* would have gone on to clarify the role of the crowd factor in other areas of change.

For all its anti-hierarchical and egalitarian thrust, Canetti's image of the crowd is still ambivalent in a fundamental respect. This becomes obvious if we link the first and last of the defining features. The crowd *has* a direction in the simple sense that it tends to grow, but it also *"needs a direction"* (*CP*, 32) of a more specific kind, and this need may be fulfilled by external actors. The goal-directedness of the crowd is, in other words, both essential to its independent life and conducive to absorption or takeover by other social forces. Canetti seems to be thinking of this ambiguity when — somewhat cryptically — he refers to "another tendency hidden in the crowd, which appears to lead to new and superior kinds of formation," often of an unpre-dictable kind (*CP*, 33). In that sense, the crowd is both an autonomous expression and an adaptable resource of social creativity.

Power and Its Transformations

According to Canetti, it is only with the French Revolution that the crowd takes on "a form which we feel to be modern" and appears "in its nakedness, in what one might call its biological state, without the transcendental theo-ries and goals which used to be inculcated in it" (*CP*, 23). This is his clearest statement about the distinctive features of modernity, and the analysis of interconnections between crowd formations and other modern phenomena is obviously an important part of his project, even if this intention often seems lost in a maze of detours. But the scope of crowd theory is universal, and one of its most sweeping claims is indicated in a late aphorism: Canetti is, as he puts it, more and more convinced that "convictions arise from crowd experiences" (*GU,* 24). This extreme emphasis on crowds is not altogether unproblematic for an author who can also write that "public life robs a person of his integrity" (*GU,* 11), and who reserves his greatest admiration for paradigmatic outsiders like Burckhardt and Stendhal. (It should, however, be noted that his most detested intellectual adversary was another great outsider: Friedrich Nietzsche.) Canetti seems particularly interested in two starkly opposite examples of the human condition, the uncontrolled crowd and the solitary creator; what they have in common is the effort to transcend human finitude.

But Canetti's interest in archaic and alien parts of the "human province" is not simply a sign of universalist ambition. It reflects a very peculiar attitude to the modern world: the conviction that "a modern man has nothing to add to modernity, if only because he has nothing to oppose it with" (*GU,* 79). Since a more adequate understanding of modernity is *eo ipso* an addition to it, we may take this to apply to theoretical no less than to artistic projects. A modern man who wants to understand his own world must transcend his modern identity (the ability to do so exemplifies the more general self-transformative competence that Canetti sees as the very core of human nature), and that means drawing on the experiences and achievements of other worlds on both sides of the conventional divide between primitive and civilized humanity. If this relativization of modern perspectives is to be effective, the otherness opposed to it should be as diverse as possible, and "spurious unities" should not affect our perception of it; this is particularly true of the variegated but far too often ignored primitive world.

In contrast to the pointedly modern context of the introductory discussion of the crowd, references to pre-modern and primitive conditions become predominant as Canetti goes on to analyze other — directly or indirectly related — aspects of human reality. His reflections on power take the same general line, although their specific connections with preceding themes are not always clear. The question of power is raised somewhat abruptly after a lengthy survey of crowds and packs of various kinds; it may be possible to show that the power factor is implicitly involved in the formation and functioning of those social bodies, but we must first disentangle the main threads of Canetti's explicit theorizing. His comments on the "entrails," "aspects," and "elements" of power will seem less impressionistic if they can be related to developments within the sociological universe of discourse.

To summarize a complex issue, one of the most telling objections to the dominant image of society has to do with its inadequate account of the role of power in social life; a simplified and sanitized notion of power has accompanied the idealized models of normative order and systemic unity. The reconceptualization of power is one of the major unfinished tasks of contemporary social theory, and Canetti's unorthodox approach is at least a useful reminder of unsolved problems. A brief survey of recent and contemporary attempts to rethink power will help to put his ideas into perspective. The starting point — and the common target of criticism — is a notion of power that was perhaps most clearly defined by Max Weber in his well-known discussion of basic sociological concepts. (It should, of course, be seen as a preliminary account of conventional assumptions, rather than a guide to Weber's own historical and sociological analyses.) It is best described as subject-centered and interactionist: power is the capacity of an actor to determine the conduct of another actor, "even against resistance." Among the critical responses to it, three main lines of argument can be distinguished. The first proposes a broader and more diversifiable concept of power. Most important, it is to be extended beyond the domain of interhuman relations and applied to the relationship between man and nature. Anthony Giddens's definition of power as the transformative capacity of human action and his distinction between allocative and authoritative resources of power (the former related to mastery over nature, the latter to domination within society) is the most obvious example. But the more comprehensive concept is also more open to differentiation: this line of thought lends itself to the theorizing of disguised or sublimated power in various areas of human life, and thus to a critique of supposedly neutral patterns of technical, organizational or cognitive rationality. The second strategy differs from the first one in that it aims at a more basic conceptual reorientation, rather than an expansion and completion of existing models. The analysis of power is to focus on trans-subjective networks and configurations, there is a stronger emphasis on the anonymity and impersonal dynamic of power structures, and their impact on the conditions and contexts of action becomes more important than the direct causal effect highlighted in Weber's definition; this relational view contrasts with the more traditional and commonsense conception of power as possessed by an actor, exercised over other actors, and visible to both sides. Michel Foucault's work on power is no doubt the most influential recent attempt to theorize along these lines, but Norbert Elias's earlier treatment of the same theme is arguably more important. Finally, the historical sociology of power has drawn attention to long-term transformations that cannot be adequately understood within the framework of traditional theories; the changes and connections involved go beyond the limits of a subject-centered perspective. In this context, Elias's work on state formation and the civilizing process is of particular importance. It centers on three main dimensions of change: the progressive pacification of social life, linked to the monopolization of violence by the state; changing relationships and proportions between different forms of social power, especially the economic and political ones; and the gradual, far-reaching but intrinsically incomplete replacement of external controls by internal ones. Further discussion of these trends is beyond the scope of the present chapter, but they may be seen as typical of the field of inquiry opened up by the third strategy.

As I will now try to show, Canetti's reflections on power reveal a distinctive approach to each of these three problematics, and they suggest a similarly distinctive way of linking them to each other. With regard to the first line of rethinking, Canetti shares with many others the view that our ideas about power make too much of its sociocultural surface and should be revised in the light of basic but neglected facts about the relationship between man and nature. But his reconstruction of primary patterns of power does not start with transformative capacity or productive activity; however essential these aspects of human conduct may be for the pursuit of mastery over nature, they are — as Canetti sees it — superimposed on more elementary constellations that open up more interesting perspectives on power. This substratum has to do with the body and its interaction with its natural environment. Here power appears in its most primitive, straightforward, and undisguisedly destructive form: if the grip of the hand is the "central and most often celebrated act of power" (*CP*, 240), incorporation through "assimilation to the body of the eater . . . may very well be seen as the central, if most hidden process of power" (*CP*, 246). But there is another side to the bodily dynamics of power. In striving to maximize speed as well as other aspects of power, "man took animals for his models" (*CP*, 329), and even inorganic natural phenomena — most famously lightning — could be perceived as symbols of supreme power, to be imitated by humans on a more modest scale. It is the receptivity and adaptability of the body as a mutable part of nature that makes it capable of modeling power.

These elementary patterns give rise to higher-level projections. Once again, the imagination appears as a crucial but covert part of the picture: its role in the extrapolation and transfiguration of power relations is never theorized. Imaginary factors are obviously involved in the transfer of models from primary processes between man and nature to more complex structures of domination within the human world; that applies to "the despot who reduces men to animals and only manages to rule them by regarding them as belonging to a lower species" (*CP*, 420), as well as to the self-image of man as opposed to myriad inferior creatures, in which Canetti sees "the exact model of the dynamics of power" (*CP*, 420). The latter vision reflects the experience of human self-assertion against nature and animates the drive for exorbitant power over other humans. Canetti thus highlights the two most important — and interrelated — correctives to over-rationalized notions of power: the links to animal life and the phantasms that draw on primal sources to transcend all instrumental or functional logic. The avoidance of conceptual integration — and, in particular, the failure to theorize the imagination — does not prevent him from making insightful connections between the natural foundations and the cultural formations of power. No other analyst of power has matched his ability to bring together the extremes of brutality and refinement. Frequent reminders of the "threat of death" as "the coin of power" (*CP*, 547) are accompanied by efforts to uncover the dynamics of power behind the most elaborate and least transparent constructs. The performance of an orchestral conductor is a case in point: from the conventional point of view it is all service and interpretation, but to Canetti it reveals all attributes of power and exemplifies the link between bodily postures and the exercise of authority (*CP*, 458–60). Another example is the transformation of the logic of question and answer into a mechanism of control: "The most blatant tyranny is the one which asks the most blatant questions" (*CP*, 332), and the institutions of cross-examination and police registration are only standardized versions of a much more comprehensive pattern.

It should be noted that Canetti's archaeology of power throws new light on some key conceptual distinctions. Multiple and contrasting aspects were characteristic of power from the outset, and they are open to further elaboration; the differences noted by theorists of power can thus be traced back to unacknowledged origins. Canetti accepts the distinction between force and power as a relevant one, but the reference to its archaic roots changes its meaning. It is the extension in space and time that raises brute force to the level of power (*CP*, 327); this opens up the possibility of indirect control as well as deferred action, but mastery over space and time can also lead to compression and acceleration, and the ability to revert to brute force remains essential to power. Similar things can be said about the distinction between operative and representative aspects of power. Even at the most elementary level, there is a difference between the "thousand tricks of power which are enacted above ground" and the underlying reality of "digestion and again digestion" (*CP*, 246); this separation of the visible from the invisible is the natural foundation for further symbolization and self-representation of power, and the symbolic context is in turn the precondition for rationalizing and legitimizing constructs. But there is a further disturbing twist to Canetti's reflections: "Power at its core and apex . . . is sufficient unto itself and wills only itself. This is the peak of its glory and, to this very day, it seems as though there were nothing which could prevent its reappearance in the same form" (*CP*, 241). He is, in other words, suggesting that the self-assertion of naked power — the discarding of rationalizing and legitimizing conventions — might have a legitimizing effect sui generis: not that the superimposed trappings are simply redundant, but the act of rising above them and reverting to the primal essence of power has an appeal of its own, unaffected by historical changes and undiminished by apparent triumphs of reason and civilization.

This view is clearly inspired by the twentieth-century experience of total power. That background is even more obviously relevant to Canetti's treatment of the second theme outlined above: the broadening of our perspectives on power beyond the interactionist frame of reference. In contemporary social theory this line of thought is above all reflected in a stronger emphasis on impersonal and anonymous aspects of power: networks, structures, apparatuses and configurations have been analyzed from various angles and in more or less explicit opposition to subject-centered theories. Canetti is, of course, not unaware of such issues. He notes the sublimation of power into functioning apparatuses: when we use the language of function and utility, "we mean by this that some process is completely and undisturbedly within our power" (*CP*, 243). And although he refuses to theorize culture as a complement and counterweight to power, his comments on specific cases are often insightful. Both the power effect of entrenched cultural patterns, such as the Aristotelian organization of knowledge (*PM*, 46–47) and the cultural paradigms of commanding power, exemplified by the Roman legacy (*PM*, 43–44), are subjected to criticism.[20] But Canetti's most original and important contribution has to do with another face of power: a trans-subjective dynamic which manifests itself in the transformation and isolation (or, as Canetti likes to put it, the "onliness") of the power-wielder. In contrast to the impersonal mechanisms analyzed by mainstream theory, the focus is here on a manifest hyper-personalization of power that can, however, be understood as an expression of more fundamental forces.

For further clarification of this point, we must return to Canetti's account of the human condition. Power, death and survival are intimately interconnected; if "the moment of *survival* is the moment of power" (*CP*, 265), it is because it represents a vicarious triumph over death and thus an imaginary transgression of absolute limits. The pursuit and exercise of power is inherent in life itself; mortality dooms it to ultimate failure, but the experience of the death of others is a double-edged confirmation of this basic fact of life: those who survive can enjoy a "secret triumph" (*GW*, 27) over the threat that has been diverted to other targets. This inescapable ambiguity of the ultimate human experience can develop into an open quest for power through survival. When Canetti claims that man "wants to kill so that he can survive others" (*CP*, 293), he is not referring to an irresistible and undeviating drive, but to a temptation inherent in the human condition, richly documented in records of the past and in no way neutralized by the real but precarious pacification of social life. For Canetti, it is of crucial importance that efforts to satisfy the desire for survival — and for the distinction that it confers — can lead to accumulation of personal power to amass and destroy as well as to sublimation into the impersonal power of structures and function. Warlords and conquerors achieve survival on a mass scale, not only by destroying their enemies, but also by sacrificing their troops; war is, however, not the only way for power-wielders to pursue this goal, and if we want to decipher the meaning of more roundabout strategies, we must take due notice of the most aberrant and manifestly pathological cases. Canetti's analysis of the Indian sultan who decided to empty his capital of its inhabitants (*CP*, 493–505) and his diagnosis of Daniel Schreber (*CP*, 505–37) are exemplary reminders of the latter point. Paranoia, recorded in a uniquely lucid fashion by Schreber, is for Canetti "an *illness of power* in the most literal sense of the words" (*CP*, 520), and this claim has a twofold meaning: paranoia reveals the pathological bent of power, and it is an affliction to which power-wielders are constitutively prone. What we can learn from both cases is that "the act of power can consist in *removing* others" (*CP*, 23), and not only in the most direct and brutal sense — imaginary annihilation is also an act of power. And what the case of Schreber highlights is the duality of the paranoid vision: the phantasm of being alone in the world after the destruction of all other human beings represents the "most extreme phase of power" (*GW*, 40), but its obverse is the delusion of absorbing multitudes of disembodied souls. Schreber's model was based on a neat separation of soul and body, but the same double-edged procedure is at work in the less orderly projects of effective power-wielders. They pursue "onliness" through the destruction as well as through the reduction and appropriation of others; the latter act aims at degrading human beings to instruments and resources of power, and thus at the abolition of human plurality, even if not on the physical level. This union of destruction and absorption is, as Canetti argues, foreshadowed in the primitive belief that a warrior can incorporate the souls or vital forces of his slain enemies.

It should be noted that the thrust of Canetti's reflections on the phantasm of "onliness" and the structural madness of power is ontological rather than psychological: he formulates his thesis in terms of tensions, tendencies, and potentialities of the human condition, reflected in the behavioral patterns of individuals. In that sense, we can speak of transsubjective forces operating through the ostensibly self-elevating subject; they result in the projection of power beyond plurality and the concomitant elimination of otherness. To put it this way is — in a broad sense — to propose a phenomenological reading of Canetti, and also to indicate the general direction of a possible phenomenological critique: its main task would consist in broadening the reference to the human condition beyond the exclusive focus on death and survival. A brief and ambiguous remark on Schreber, defused in the English text, might serve as the starting point for such a critique: "Of his own human body Schreber often speaks as though it were a world body" (*CP*, 506; translation amended: Canetti's term is *Weltkörper,* and "world body" seems more adequate than "celestial body" — it refers to a situation where the body tends to become coextensive with the world). The phenomenological concept of the world could be used to spell out the implications of this statement.

The twin imaginary institutions of omnicompetent apparatus and omnipotent leader (interrelated, but not always equally developed) are characteristic of totalitarian regimes, and the latter has proved more difficult to theorize than the former. Canetti's analyses can therefore be read as an essential corrective to more orthodox approaches. But his attempt to make sense of the totalitarian phenomenon is also relevant to the third part of our problematic: the historical transformations of power. In this regard, totalitarian power is a particularly challenging case. On the one hand, the radical novelty of its aims and methods has been noted by many analysts and has made the question of historical origins highly controversial; on the other hand, the break with established traditions was accompanied and exacerbated by developments that seemed more easily explainable as throwbacks to archaic conditions. Various theories of totalitarianism have tried to account for this destructive symbiosis of innovation and regression (for example, Adorno and Horkheimer saw it as a self-defeating triumph of structurally impoverished and therefore regressive reason).

Canetti tackles this question in a very distinctive way. The Nazi phenomenon — with Hitler at its center — is his prime example of totalitarian power, and it is possible to read the whole text of *Crowds and Power* as a prolegomenon to more direct treatment of this event that "defied understanding."[21] The reference to Hitler as a "Mongol Prince" who conquered Europe and came "within a hair's breadth of the conquest of the world" (*CP*, 519) shows how seriously Canetti took the most manifestly premodern aspects of totalitarianism. In his view, mass murder and wholesale destruction had become ends in themselves on an unprecedented scale, and those who tried to reduce them to by-products of structural or ideological factors were missing the essence of the phenomenon. But Canetti's interpretation differs from more common ways of theorizing the archaic in that it does not depend on evolutionary assumptions. Those who stressed the similarities between twentieth-century totalitarianism and earlier forms of tyranny or barbarism were mostly inclined to explain them as the result of reversals or self-destructive turns of long-term transformations; the latter could be conceptualized as civilizing or rationalizing processes, but there was at least a limited acceptance of evolutionary models, whereas Canetti wants to do without them (at any rate with regard to the problem discussed here; it does not follow that his approach excludes all kinds of long-term processes). The return to unalloyed and unmitigated violence, reinforced by resources developed in the course of movement beyond it, is — as suggested above — one of the elementary patterns of power and should therefore be treated as a recurrent feature of history as such, rather than a regressive outcome of specific developments. But if it is repeated on an enlarged scale in the modern world, this must be due to historically novel conditions.

For Canetti, these conditions have — above all else — to do with the unprecedented strength and salience of modern crowd formations. In contrast to conventional wisdom about the dependence of crowds on power, he stresses the problematic relationship between the two sides and its specifically modern vicissitudes. From the perspective of those who pursue or exercise power, the more dynamic and autonomous crowds represent new challenges as well as new possibilities; the arrangements that serve to control and mobilize modern crowds enrich the armory of power, but they can also maximize the effect of its most primal and destructive elements. For Canetti, this is the key to the totalitarian phenomenon. The totalitarian power-wielder (*Machthaber*) as a conqueror, creator, stage-manager and destroyer of crowds is the ultimate embodiment of the forces that previously came to the fore in archaic excesses and pathological phantasms. Canetti's brilliant essay on Hitler is the most conclusive presentation of this line of thought. Hitler's addiction to power and his compulsion to outdo models and rivals (*GW*, 177) acquired a more specific content through his obsession with crowds. His project encompassed crowds aroused by demagogy, mobilized for war, massacred on the battlefield, or liquidated as victims of the new order; the unifying principle is the phantasm of a perfect and permanent absorption of crowds by power. Canetti did not write about Stalin, but it might be possible to construct a comparable model — centered on the mobilization and liquidation of crowds — for the Stalinist phase of Soviet totalitarianism.

The Anthropological Agenda

I have discussed Canetti's two main themes at some length; a systematic interpretation of *Crowds and Power* is beyond the scope of this chapter, but some concluding remarks on less-developed aspects of Canetti's image of man and society may be useful. They will deal with categories and phenomena that exemplify the interconnections between crowds and power, as well as with the question of possible counterweights to these two determinants of the human condition.

Canetti raises the question of power somewhat abruptly after devoting more than a third of the text to other matters, and he does not explain why it should be posed at this particular point. A closer reading suggests that the power factor is in fact implicitly taken into account in the analysis of various crowd-related or crowd-inducing phenomena. This applies to the discussion of religions and their efforts to domesticate the crowd (*CP*, 26–28): if crowd management through closure and controlled growth is one of the essential functions of religion, it obviously involves the specific power of religious institutions, and the inadequacy of that power in relation to modern crowds is one of the reasons for the rise of new power-wielders. Power is also one of the constitutive components of "crowd crystals"; this is Canetti's term for "small, rigid groups of men, strictly delimited and of great constancy, which serve to precipitate crowds" (*CP*, 85), and his choice of soldiers and monks as the main examples highlights the role of power. There is no detailed inventory of crowd crystals, but it seems legitimate to conclude that institutions of various kinds — or groups which represent them — can function as crowd crystals in appropriate circumstances.

Power is, in short, less external to the world of the crowd and its offshoots than a first glance might lead us to believe. It is an omnipresent and multifaceted aspect of the human condition, and even the description of the open crowd at the very beginning reflects its limited and ambiguous escape from the domain of power. But the tacit reference to power is particularly important in the case of the pack. This is one of Canetti's key concepts, and his discussion of it (*CP*, 109–93) would merit a detailed commentary; in the present context, we can only note some basic points. The pack, defined as "a group of men in a state of excitement whose fiercest wish is to be more" (*CP*, 109) and "all obsessed by the same goal" (*CP*, 110), is the historical ancestor of both crowds and crowd crystals; it is the basic unit of primitive societies (as we have seen, Canetti does not follow the Durkheimian model that would have led him to distinguish between pack and crowd within the primitive world) and the origin of more complex formations. Canetti's analysis of the pack is perhaps best understood as a rejoinder to the classical interpretation of social structures in terms of cooperation and division of labor (and, by implication, to those who have translated this paradigm into more abstract language). This will become clearer if we consider the rational and functional aspects of the pack: they are crucial to its cohesion and continuity but inextricably intermingled with other traits of a very different kind. The pack is purposively rational in that it is collectively oriented towards a clearly defined goal, but at the same time its activity is sustained by excitement and obsession. It seems obvious — although Canetti does not elaborate on this — that the emotional factor transfigures the goal-rationality of the pack into a struggle against adversaries or adverse conditions, and in so doing makes the power component more explicit. Similarly, the functional determinacy of the pack — its unfailing adaptation to a specific task — is accompanied and relativized by a negative characteristic: there is always "the wish to be more," the awareness of a discrepancy between the incumbent task and the available force. The pack is, in other words, a defective crowd and perceives itself as such; as Canetti puts it, only two features of the crowd — equality and direction — are fully present, whereas the other two — growth and density — are "desired and enacted" (*CP*, 110). Since the pack is by definition engaged in a struggle against its environment, the lack of crowd resources means a lack of power. Functional performance is undermined by a power deficit, and at the same time overlaid by imaginary compensations for this shortcoming. This internal fracture of the pack might be seen as the most elementary expression of the difference between instituted and instituting aspects of social being.

Canetti distinguishes four basic forms and functions of the pack. The parallel with Parsons's well-known four-function scheme is intriguing, but there is no acknowledged connection. If we compare the interpretive contents, the Parsonian functions and corresponding subdivisions of the social (which I cannot discuss here) are variations on the theme of control, whereas Canetti's four types are variations on the theme of conflict. This is self-evident in the first two cases: the hunting pack and the war pack are agencies of the struggle for survival (in the conventional as well as in the Canettian sense), and in view of Canetti's emphasis on continuities between the animal and human worlds, the power used to kill animals and other humans is essentially of the same kind (the main difference being, of course, that the war pack is always confronted with another pack). As for the third type, the lamenting pack that "forms when a member of a group is torn from it by death" (*CP*, 112), its function can only be understood in connection with Canetti's claim that the naturalization of death — its acceptance as part of the natural order of things — was a relatively late and long-drawn-out development, due in large measure to the world religions. From this point of view, the primitive lamenting pack (reactivated by some religions for their own purposes) must be seen as a response to and a protest against the most challenging aspect of the human condition. Finally, the increase pack is "formed so that the group itself, or the living beings, whether plants or animals, with which it is associated, should become more" (*CP*, 112). Here the collective effort is directed against an all-round shortage of resources that hampers the human confrontation with nature. For Canetti, this function is specific enough to set the fourth type apart from the others, but it should not be identified with more particular ends or means. Ritual and rational action, population growth and technological progress, accumulation of useful objects and productive potential all belong to its historical domain. The increase pack represents "the desire to be more" on a more general level than the other types, and in that capacity, it has "conquered the earth . . . and led to ever richer civilizations" (*CP*, 125). Canetti's insistence on its early origins reflects his dissatisfaction with two other approaches to primitive society: the model of a self-maintaining equilibrium as well as the over-generalized and anachronistic conception of the productive forces as the motor of human history from the beginning.

According to Canetti, "all forms of pack . . . have a tendency to change into one another" (*CP*, 149), and the transformations undergone, engineered and imagined by the increase pack are of particular importance (*CP*, 126). Here we encounter Canetti's notion of transformation, tantalizingly underdeveloped but central to his whole intellectual project and therefore the most appropriate starting point for some concluding remarks.[22] The power of transformation is the "specific gift" of man (*CP*, 237) and the source of human "power over all other creatures" (*CP,* 389). We have already dealt with some of its major manifestations: the crowd experience can only be understood as a transformation, and the same applies to the multiple modalities of power. But it is easier to note the presence of the power of transformation than to theorize its nature and potential. Canetti frequently refers to it as a mystery or a hidden source of all human achievements and creations. In an early aphorism, he speaks — probably in a self-critical vein — of the danger that the theory of transformation might "become a panacea before it is fully thought out" (*PM,* 49). It is certainly true that he often invoked the concept without doing much to develop it. An attempt to go further might start with the observation that Canetti needed a keyword to emphasize difference and diversity as fundamental but often forgotten characteristics of the human world. When he criticizes "most philosophers" for having "too little sense of the variability of human customs and possibilities" (*PM,* 36), the complaint is — by implication — directed against historians and social scientists as well. Canetti is, in other words, raising an issue that critics of identitarian logic and metaphysics have tackled from another angle; from his point of view, they made the mistake of posing the problem in terms that already conceded too much to the conceptual imperialism of the adversary and failed to grasp the anthropological counterweight to identity. (He does not discuss Adorno's concept of mimesis, but it seems likely that he would have seen it as a philosophically preprocessed and therefore inferior alternative.) The notion of transformation is geared to the latter task. If we want to specify its potential uses, it may be most helpful to treat it as a condensed reference to ideas that have been developed in other contexts under different headings and with varying success.

There is, to begin with, an obvious affinity between the notion of transformation and the idea of the self-defining and self-transforming subject. The latter (analyzed most convincingly by Charles Taylor) has been a central theme in modern thought and culture. It lends itself to a variety of constructions, but at least one line of interpretation stresses the ability to create and change identities, which is also central to Canetti's account of man's "transforming nature." (He is, however, no less aware of the fact that this competence can be turned against itself — the effort to absolutize identities and protect them against change is the obverse of transforming activity, and the "specific gift" can easily be perceived as an internal threat.) At the same time, Canetti rejects the modern understanding and usage of transformation as self-centered and therefore blind to the most creative manifestations of the same potential in previous historical epochs. The interpretive key that he uses to open up broader perspectives is a good example of the effort to transcend modernity so as to understand it better: a return to mythology is expected to bring new insights into the nature of transformation.[23] But the conception of mythology as — above all else — a narrative of transformation is based on a particular historical source. It reflects a late interpretation of classical mythology, most effectively and influentially codified in Ovid's *Metamorphoses* (one of Canetti's most favored texts, although he applies its main idea more systematically to primitive than to classical mythology).

The use of myths to elucidate the notion of transformation is — implicitly — another acknowledgment of the imaginary background to all human efforts and experiences. Canetti's treatment of this subject shows clearly that he is interested in the manifest contents of the mythopoeic imagination, rather than any latent meanings, but the reluctance to conceptualize the imagination is no less evident than in relation to crowds and power.[24] On the other hand, the projected theory of transformation tells us something about the broader context in which an anthropological analysis of the imagination should be grounded. Most important, the "talent for transformation" affects and enriches human relations with the world: the ability to conceive of and identify with other beings, animate or inanimate, is inseparable from self-transformative capacity, and this connection is most forcefully articulated in primitive mythology. It is, in Canetti's view, an essential aspect of totemic religion, although it has been misunderstood or overlooked by analysts of that phenomenon (from Durkheim to Lévi-Strauss). But an even earlier and therefore more revealing form of the fusion of man and world can be found in Bushman folklore; Canetti describes a book on this subject as "our most valuable record on early humanity" (*CP*, 389). What makes this text so important is not that it proves the existence of primordial human faculties that we have lost (Canetti prefers to reserve judgment on this point), but that it exemplifies the most basic mechanisms of transformation, which have to do with the bodily unity of self-perception and perception of the other.

Canetti deals with these remote origins at greater length than with later stages, but he makes it clear that the "transforming nature" of man is the source of very diverse developments: as he sees it, man owes both his power and his compassion to transformation (*GW*, 245). But there is more to be said on the specific and complex relationship between power and transformation. As we have seen, power uses transformation for its own purposes; in a more fundamental sense, power is a natural enemy of transformation, both because it is "sufficient unto itself and wills only itself" (*CP*, 241) and because it "wages continuous warfare against spontaneous and uncontrolled transformation" (*CP*, 438). Prohibitions on transformation — from religious taboos to caste systems — are therefore an essential part of power structures. On the other hand, it seems — although this theme is only marginally present in *Crowds and Power* — that transformation can impose its own logic on power, and in so doing open up a new dimension of the human world. The hand is analyzed as the primary instrument of power, but its "quiet, prolonged activities" have also "created the only world in which we care to live" (*CP*, 249). On the basis of speculations about the role of the hand in the genesis of sign language, Canetti concludes that both words and objects are ultimately products of representation by the hands. This is followed by a very far-reaching thesis: "Everything that a man can do, everything that represents his culture, he first incorporated into himself by means of transformation" (*CP*, 254). Here Canetti uses the concept of culture, which he elsewhere rejects (and which otherwise plays no role in *Crowds and Power*), to describe the outcome of a transformation that we might call the civilizing of power.

This transformation involves a reorientation of power in its most elementary form. But Canetti also hints at civilizing changes of a more complex kind. The Chinese tradition is credited with having invented the "figure of the ideal power-wielder" (*CP*, 317) — the English text uses the word "ruler," but Canetti's term is *Machthaber*, which is elsewhere — and more adequately — translated as "power-wielder"). The allusion to Confucian thought becomes even clearer when Canetti goes on to praise the Chinese version of ancestor worship for having in some respects changed "the character of survival" (*CP*, 316) by purging it of crowd characteristics and merging piety towards the dead with awareness of self. The thrust of this argument is unmistakable: it is the existential core of power, the experience of survival, that is given a new and mitigating meaning. When Canetti says about Confucius that he "ignores the nature of power, its innermost core" (*GW*, 201) and is only interested in certain ways of using it, he is clearly thinking of a civilizing project. But was the intention to transform power incompatible with study of its nature? Canetti seems to think so: "It is very strange that all thinkers in human history who understand something about the facts of power *approve* of it. The thinkers who are *against* power scarcely grasp its essence" (*GW*, 201). If we take this statement at face value, *Crowds and Power* is the first attempt to bridge the gap between the two traditions.

It is, to say the least, not self-evident that a voluntary ignorance of the workings of power could have helped to create the models that Canetti finds so admirable. But this puzzle is only one aspect of a more general problem. Canetti leaves us with ambiguous statements and open questions about the relationship between culture and power, and his rejection of traditional concepts compounds the difficulties. This is not to deny that it might be possible to extract further clues from his work. That task is, however, beyond the scope of the present work. Its purpose is a more limited one: to build conceptual bridges between Canetti's unique intellectual universe and the discursive community of social theory. At this point, we can attempt only a provisional summing-up, and Canetti's own judgment on Jacob Burckhardt might be the best formula for it: "One need not accept him. One cannot dismiss him" (*GU,* 10).

5: The Subversive Sources of Power

CANETTI'S APHORISMS (to use the widely accepted but not fully adequate English translation of *Aufzeichnungen*) are very directly related to his work on *Crowds and Power*. His own account of the connection sounds rather dismissive: he describes the aphorisms as a "safety valve" that enabled him to concentrate on the main project without risking exhaustion and paralysis. The sheer volume and continuity of the aphorisms — they chronicle Canetti's thought over half a century — would seem to suggest more significant aims. Even a cursory reading will show that Canetti was experimenting with several interconnected lines of reflection. But the following discussion will focus on one of them: the question to be pursued is whether the aphorisms contain elements or adumbrations of a theory of culture that would match his main concern, the theory of power. For this purpose, *The Human Province* is a key text. The question must, however, be posed with major qualifications in mind. It goes without saying that the term "theory" is being used in a very flexible sense, not to be confused with closed systems or nomological constructions; this is in line with a more general trend, exemplified by the shift from sociological to social theory. Canetti's reflections, however unconventional in style and content, are no less relevant to the agenda of social theory than the more widely debated heterodoxies of the last two or three decades: it will, for example, become apparent that his thought has some latent points of contact with the work of Cornelius Castoriadis. But it is more difficult to interpret him as a theorist of culture than as a theorist of power. He uses the concept of power, but rejects the concept of culture; a major detour will therefore be needed to link his insights to the problematic commonly centered on the latter. This conceptual asymmetry is compounded by differences between the texts. References to *Crowds and Power* will help to clarify the more radically anti-systematic discourse of *The Human Province*.

Learning from Hobbes

There can be no better starting-point for the proposed inquiry than Canetti's long comment on Hobbes in *The Human Province*, dated 1949. As he puts it, Hobbes is "at the moment" the most important of the thinkers who broke free of religion and took the resultant insights to extremes. "He is the only thinker I know of who does not disguise power, its weight and its central role in all human behavior; but he does not glorify it, he simply lets it stand as it is" (*PM*, 153). As we shall see, this uniquely unprejudiced focus on power is not unproblematic. But before going on to discuss the criticisms Canetti made, it is worth noting that his reference to Hobbes as a landmark thinker is comparable to the views of several major twentieth-century theorists. Hobbes seems particularly well suited for the role of a provocative pioneer whose insights set new standards but fell far short of full comprehension. A brief glance at key examples may help to put Canetti's particular variation on this theme in perspective.

Hannah Arendt's interpretation of Hobbes is perhaps the most clearly kindred case. She did not locate the central problem at the anthropological level indicated by Canetti, but her main emphasis was nevertheless on a new understanding of power: she credited Hobbes with an intuitive grasp of power in its distinctively bourgeois form; that is, as abstract and therefore intrinsically expansive power, corresponding to the abstract wealth that became the telos of capitalist development.[1] Hobbes's analysis of this phenomenon, undertaken two centuries before Marx explored the dynamics of abstract wealth, did not extend to its historical context. The anthropological perspective thus appears as an incomplete version of a historical one. Arendt nevertheless argued that Hobbes's vision of the cumulative pursuit of power anticipated the logic of totalitarianism.

Among the twentieth-century attempts to link a re-reading of Hobbes to new perspectives on man and society, the argument put forward by Talcott Parsons is surely most familiar to social theorists: for him, Hobbes exemplified both an uncompromising grasp of the problem of social order and a radically misconceived (purely strategic) solution to it. His focus on order is starkly opposed to Canetti's approach; there is hardly a more pronounced contrast within the spectrum of twentieth-century social thought. For a more congenial case, we may turn to Leo Strauss's early work on Hobbes. For Strauss, Hobbes was an epoch-making figure because he was the "founder of modern political philosophy," a philosophy based on a conception of natural law that starts from "a series of 'rights' — of subjective claims, originating in the human will,"[2] and a closer examination of his thought was able to show that this view was prior to any significant contact with modern science (although Hobbes subsequently tried to align his political thought with what he took to be the immanent philosophy of modern science). Hobbes is, in other words, the thinker who articulated "the deepest stratum of the modern mind" and did so in "the fertile moment when the classical and theological tradition was already shaken and a tradition of modern science not yet formed and established."[3] This assessment converges with Canetti's understanding of Hobbes as a thinker who made a particularly radical break with religion. But Strauss later changed his mind and came to think that Machiavelli, rather than Hobbes, was the main originator of modern political philosophy. As we shall see, Canetti's reflections have some bearing on that claim.

For present purposes, the chapter on Hobbes in Franz Borkenau's work on the origins of the modern worldview is perhaps the most interesting example. Borkenau's broader project was a re-examination of the transition from feudal to bourgeois societies and a revision of conventional Marxist views on that subject. His reference to the seventeenth century as one of the darkest periods in human history, characterized by the loss of religious faith and the persistence of religious fear, points beyond the historical materialism to which he still subscribed when he wrote the book; the implications became more apparent with his later turn to civilizational theory. His treatment of Hobbes reflects the ambiguity of a paradigm shift in the making. On the one hand, the Marxist approach leads to reductionistic explanations of Hobbes's ideas in terms of class interests and historical conjunctures (he appears as a spokesman of the conservative bourgeoisie during the seventeenth-century English revolution). On the other hand, he interprets the same ideas as visions of the social world and the human condition, far too universal in scope and content to fit into the historical-materialist model. Contrasts and parallels with Canetti become apparent in this context. For Hobbes, as read by Borkenau, the pursuit of wealth is "a part of the will to power,"[4] as is the quest for honor; this fusion of economic and political man results in the most consistent formulation of the principles "homo homini lupus" and "bellum omnium contra omnes" (a war of all against all, due to the natural mutual enmity of human beings) as natural laws of social behavior. But the final and crowning conclusion is the affirmation of "the presence of rationality in pure violence."[5] More precisely, rationality prevails on two levels: through the insight into the motive forces and recurrent patterns of human actions, and through the law imposed by the sovereign absolute ruler. The "phantom of the wise ruler"[6] represents the final reconciliation of right and power. From Canetti's point of view, this reading would seem to unmask Hobbes as — in the last instance — an apologist of power.

Canetti's own interpretation should now be examined more closely, and we may begin with his reasons for preferring Hobbes to Machiavelli. He begins by dismissing Machiavelli as "hardly a half, the classical half" (*PM*, 154) of Hobbes. This would be in line with the conventional view that Hobbes grasped the logic of modern statehood in the making, whereas Machiavelli took the narrower horizons of city-states for granted. But the next observation is more original: Thucydides is for Hobbes what Livius was for Machiavelli. Now it is no longer a question of one thinker staying within classical boundaries and the other moving beyond them; rather, the two cases represent different aspects and uses of the classical legacy. The contrast between Thucydides and Livius must be understood in light of Canetti's more general reflection on historians and their characteristic preconceptions. As he sees it, the most absurd of all religions, "the religion of power" (*PM*, 41), has also been the most persistent influence on the writing and understanding of history. The paradigm that comes most naturally to historians is the story of the growth and perfecting of power. This does not necessarily mean identification with one particular power center. Ranke, to take a prominent example, was a "polytheist of power" (*PM*, 165). Livius was, of course, a straightforward case: he wrote an affirmative history of Rome's rise to unchallenged power, and his superior understanding of Roman strengths made his advocacy more persuasive than most other work in the same vein. But Thucydides is in a different category. For him, the Athenian empire was a failed project, but the tragic character of its downfall was too clear for the retreat to an untroubled "polytheism of power" to be an available option. His account of the Peloponnesian War is, if anything, even closer to the view that Canetti ascribes to Hobbes: a superior understanding of power, unhampered by traditional ways of disguising or transfiguring its dynamics.

Power, Death, and Survival

So far, the focus has been on Hobbes's strengths and achievements. For a more balanced judgment, we must now turn to Canetti's critical observations. His main objection is that Hobbes "explains everything through self-interest (*Selbstsucht*)" (*PM*, 50–51) and fails to see that this supposedly ultimate motive of human behavior is "composite" (*zusammengesetzt*) and only becomes dominant by incorporating or taking control of other parts of human nature, of which Hobbes takes no notice. The task that Canetti sets himself is to explore these neglected dimensions of the human condition. To grasp the logic of his search for a hidden complexity behind the façade of simple self-interest, it may be useful to begin with the point most closely related to mainstream critiques of Hobbes's work As we have seen, the fusion of economic and political man was central to Borkenau's reading of Hobbes, and it would be easy to find other interpretations in the same vein. Canetti does not pose the problem in conventional terms, but his reflections on power and survival are unmistakably concerned with the same issues.

A conceptual short-circuiting of power and survival is evident in Hobbes's most basic assumptions, beginning with his definition of power as "present means, to obtain some future apparent good."[7] Power thus becomes an instrument of survival in the broadest sense: as the ongoing satisfaction of needs and desires. But since all human activities, achievements, and acquisitions can serve this purpose, the pursuit of power knows no limits other than those of human life: "I put for a general inclination of all mankind, a perpetuall and restlesse desire of Power after power, that ceaseth onely in Death."[8] In the natural condition of mankind, marked by the war of every man against every man, this external limit becomes an acute threat. The constant fear and omnipresent danger of death are the main reasons why human beings opt for organized societies and accept sovereign power. In so doing, they set the stage for a new chapter in the history of power; but the sequel is beyond the scope of the present discussion.

For Canetti, power is more intimately and problematically linked to death and survival than the instrumentalist conception would have us believe. The ostensibly realistic and value-neutral conception of power as means to an end can thus be seen in a new light: it is a neutralizing device, a sanitized image that serves to screen out the most disturbing aspects of power. To be fully aware of mortality is to face ultimate disempowerment: "the slavery of death is the core of all slavery" (PM, 110–11), not only because all human beings share the fate of inescapable annihilation, but also in the more indirect sense that meanings imposed on this fate — more or less capable of mitigating its existential impact — have been at the center of beliefs and traditions that served to dignify social power. From this point of view, the experience of survival — of surviving another human being — has a double-edged meaning. It is a reminder of mortality, as well as a foretaste of power, and the latter aspect becomes more salient when survival is the result of struggle and victory. The primordial affinity of power with killing in battle has been acknowledged and glorified in different ways across the vast spectrum of human cultures. At its most extreme, this trend culminates in visions and practices of mass killing as a manifestation of power. "All famous conquerors in history have taken this road" (GW, 33). Canetti makes it clear that the claim applies to very recent experiences no less than to the traditional archetypes of conquest, and that the inherently murderous "passion of power" cannot be seen as a spent force.

This very brief summary cannot do justice to Canetti's detailed phenomenology of power and survival. However, in the present context it should suffice to indicate the distance between his perspectives and those of mainstream theorizing about power. To bridge the gap, it may be helpful to reconsider the question from an angle that relates loosely to Canetti's concerns but shifts the emphasis closer to traditional approaches. As a first step, it can be argued that the significance of power over death and life has been obscured by the generalized concept of sanctions: the importance of the ultimate sanction for the most authoritative forms of power should be underlined. But if the ability and authority to inflict death is crucial to power at its most intensive and revealing, the inability to transcend death may also be critical in the same context: an inbuilt tendency to maximize power and project its internal logic beyond all external limits would confront the ultimate limit of mortality. Seen in this way, the human pursuit of power would not only be "perpetuall and restlesse," as Hobbes put it, but inherently prone to excess, hubris and delusion. Such arguments have been put forward by some analysts of power, including those who regard phantasies of omnipotence — rooted in the psyche — as a permanent de-rationalizing factor. As we shall see, Canetti takes a distinctive line on this issue and links it to other aspects of the problem. A conflict between hubristic power and human mortality will result in the invention or imagining of perpetuating devices, more or less explicitly conceived as detours to or substitutes for immortality. It is also possible to think of mass killing, on the battlefield or elsewhere, as the most lethal of these attempts to defy death: the survivor who has destroyed human life in the grand manner can more easily cultivate the illusion of invulnerable sovereignty. The question to be asked here is whether Canetti did not link this extreme aspect of power too directly to elementary figurations; or, to put it another way, whether there is more to say on the mutations that power undergoes when it confronts and aspires to overcome the constraints built into the human condition. As we shall see, this line of interpretation links up with other themes in Canetti's work. The interrelations of power, death and survival are essential to the understanding of varieties and pathologies that reductionistic theories have tended to overlook.

But at this point, another round of reflection — on the "other domains of human nature," alluded to in Canetti's comment on Hobbes — is needed to clarify the claim that power and self-interest are composite phenomena, dependent on multiple sources and embedded in a broader context. Only a more explicit grasp of these connections can reconcile Canetti's praise of Hobbes with other statements to a seemingly contrary effect: Hobbes is ranked with De Maistre and Nietzsche as one of the great enemies (*PM,* 206), and his conception of power is to be most directly targeted for de-struction (*PM,* 176). His de-mystifying insights and descriptions would, looked at from this point of view, be vitiated by the misperception of power as a simple and ultimate datum.

Understanding Transformation

Canetti's keyword for the complexity and creative indeterminacy of human nature, seen from a distinctive angle, is "transformation" (*Verwandlung*). The questions to be posed about culture and power can be located within the orbit of this anthropological theme, and we must begin with an overview of its ramifications. At the most fundamental level, Canetti's idea of trans-formation has obvious affinities with Castoriadis's interpretation of man as "a being capable of making be other forms."[9] It is more difficult to translate the general direction into specific conceptual terms. Canetti claims to have found the key to the phenomena of transformation, and to have put it into the lock without turning it (*PM,* 249); he adds that much more work will be needed before the door can be opened. His reluctance to move from intui-tive outlines to more structured interpretations (this would have been the first turn of the key) is related to a strong antipathy to philosophical modes of thought: the philosophers have behaved like "barbarians in a tall and spacious house, full of wonderful works" (*PM,* 168), and their virtuosity in applying basic concepts has, in one way or another, led to a systematic "emptying out" (*Entleerungsprozess*) of human experience. The very medium of philosophical reflection is called into question: "The jump to the general is so dangerous that one must train it again and again, and on the same spot" (*PM,* 248). But if the most elementary step towards conceptual ar-ticulation is to be repeated ad infinitum, with constant reference to arche-typal experiences (they constitute Canetti's anthropological "spot"), the results will not go beyond preparatory moves. The keys will, in that sense, remain unturned.

Canetti's doubt about philosophy and its conceptual tools is not to be mistaken for a variant of the skepticism that has — repeatedly but inconclu-sively — challenged the philosophical tradition from within. His distrust of concepts reflects a dedicated belief in other ways and means of articulation. Among the historians who gained lasting insight into the human condition,

Burckhardt is singled out for his ability to focus on figures rather than concepts. But with regard to transformation as the "most authentic and enigmatic aspect of the human being" (*GW*, 276), literature is the main storehouse of knowledge and the prime antidote to philosophical leveling. In his "Munich Speech" of 1976 (*GW*, 272–83), Canetti describes the poet (in the broad sense of *Dichter*) as the "guardian of transformations." What he has in mind will become clearer if we consider his favorite examples. A classic account of transformations stands at the very beginning of the Western literary tradition: the *Odyssey* approaches this topic through the adventures and impersonations of an exceptional individual, but by implication also through the changing human and superhuman worlds with which he is confronted. At a much later stage of the ancient world, Ovid's *Metamorphoses* condensed the mythological universe into narratives of transformations that involved gods, heroes, humans, and non-human nature. These two "foundational books of antiquity" (*GW*, 277) have had a formative influence on modern culture, and there is no reason to believe that their reserves of meaning have been exhausted. In a sense, the transformative potential manifested in their modern offshoots is a reflexive turn to their main theme.

Canetti goes on to add a third classic to his list: a much older text with a very different history of oblivion and rediscovery, central to the world of a whole civilization (and some of its neighbors) but then thoroughly forgotten by its successors and brought back to public knowledge by remote descendants in search of a buried past. As he claims, the *Epic of Gilgamesh* has influenced his work and his way of thinking more profoundly than any other literary text. He keeps returning to it "as to a kind of bible" (*GW*, 277). It begins with the transformation of Enkidu from a natural into an urban and cultural man, and continues with Enkidu's death, which leads to Gilgamesh's confrontation with his own mortality. Two key themes of Canetti's work are thus brought to prominence and into close contact. But there is a third aspect of the epic that Canetti — very surprisingly — does not mention. The story of Gilgamesh as builder and ruler of the city of Uruk develops a theme that Canetti links most emphatically to the Chinese tradition: the humanization and civilization of power and of those who wield it. If we take this additional dimension into account, the *Epic of Gilgamesh* appears as a uniquely pioneering exploration of the human condition; no other early civilization produced anything comparable, and we can only regret that Canetti failed to elaborate on his encounter with it.

With these indications in mind, we should now define the multiple meanings and domains of transformation in more concrete terms. In light of the above caveats against premature theorizing, attempts to map out the field can only claim provisional validity, but we can at least make some elementary distinctions. It seems best to start with an emphatic statement on the inadequacy of the means-ends model integral to the mainstream of the human sciences: "For me, the authentic human being is one who does not acknowledge an end; there should be no end, and it is dangerous to invent one" (*PM*, 182). The wealth of expectations is a defining human characteristic, but it culminates in the expectation of the unexpected; "the *other* is hidden at the end of every direction" (*PM*, 182), and neither will nor knowledge can close the horizons of becoming. Here the idea of transformation is contrasted with teleological models of action, and with the corresponding conception of knowledge. The most genuine pursuit of knowledge is open to abrupt changes of perspective ("*damit es sich plötzlich anders weiss,*" *PM*, 182). For this reason, a thinker in search of new insights cannot conform to any methodical rules (*PM*, 255). The freedom and indeterminacy of original inquiry transcends all prescribed directions. But for Canetti, this general relativization of goal-oriented conduct — including the quest for certainty — carries a particular meaning. If we admit the ephemeral and illusory character of projected ends, it becomes very difficult to understand why human beings have, again and again, pursued them to the point of the highest sacrifice: laying down their lives. The paradox of human self-sacrifice, as distinctive of the species as the capacity for transformation, is central to Canetti's study of history: he wants, as he puts it, to understand everything for which human beings have been willing to die.

As an anthropological keyword, the notion of transformation casts doubt on all determinate and self-contained patterns, beginning with those of individual identity. "The human being must learn to be a plurality of beings, in a conscious fashion, and to hold them all together" (*PM,* 102); this cultivation and management of internal plurality is also a way of deflecting power from rule over others, and thus one of the civilizing devices that Canetti sees as the most acceptable human inventions. Canetti's reference to himself as "a whole primitive people" (*PM,* 186) should perhaps be understood in this context. But the same idea also serves to highlight the plurality of cultures, without mistaking them for mutually closed universes. Both the ability to transfigure the human condition into multiple worlds and the capacity to clear paths between them are rooted in the transformative potential that sets the human species apart from the rest of nature.

The original transformation that brought humanity into the cultural realm (re-enacted, as noted above, in the *Epic of Gilgamesh*) was also a prelude to an unending train of further transformations within the new dimension, and to another kind of diversity due to the quest for unity across cultural boundaries. From the transformational perspective, the new interstitial meanings emerging from cross-cultural understanding are more important than any fusion of horizons; those who seek to appropriate the wisdom of alien cultures are bound to alter its received versions by association with other contexts, and are at the same time caught up in a venture that changes their relationship to their own background. The latter aspect is not unfamiliar to analysts of cultural interaction, but Canetti's allusions to it are particularly suggestive. Seen from the distance gained through engagement with other traditions, the tacit or seemingly self-evident foundations of inherited forms of life appear in a different light. Surprising and disconcerting insights into things previously taken for granted can result from the exposure to new horizons (*NH*, 203), and in turn lead to cultural self-redefinitions that should be included in the spectrum of transformations.

The picture would be incomplete without a mention of the most utopian side to Canetti's idea of transformation. It is perhaps best understood as a vision of total and self-transcending opening to otherness, combined with a radical rejection of power: "To become a city, a whole country, a continent, without conquering anything" (*PM*, 166). Here the transformative pursuit of knowledge converges with the idea of freedom as the renunciation of power (*PM*, 170). But there is also an implicit link to his aphorisms on art and philosophy. The principle (or, to use a philosophical language that Canetti would have abhorred, the constitutive idea) of art is to rediscover more than was lost (*PM*, 147). Anamnesis and transformation are thus united in a mutually enriching way. This vision of art — and of its relation to human experience — stands out in contrast to Canetti's blanket dismissal of the philosophical tradition. The whole legacy of human history consists in the words left behind, and the philosophers seize on a few of those words at the expense of all the others (*NH*, 204). Once again, an underlying conformity with power — exercised through a leveling and immobilization of meaning — appears as the original sin of philosophical thought; in the present context, it is the significance and the consequences of this view for Canetti's anthropology that matter, rather than the question of its adequacy. The uncompromisingly elusive idea of transformation is meant to put a long-term project out of danger from desensitizing traditions.

To move closer to the crucial question of power and its relationship to transformation, some genealogical aspects may be added to the above survey of fundamentals. The chapter on transformation in *Crowds and Power* is the

most obvious starting-point for such approaches. But it is clearly one of the
least focused and integrated parts of the book: the whole discussion shows
that a new theme is being discovered and introduced alongside the more
structured problematics of crowds and power. For our purposes, it is enough
to pick out a few unequally developed ideas on the origins of processes and
figures that became central to the cultural history of power. Canetti begins
with a detailed account of apparently parapsychological phenomena among
the Bushmen, who can be seen as an exemplary case of hunting and gathering humanity in close symbiosis with nature. Romantic notions of the occult
and dismissive verdicts of superstition are — according to this view —
equally inappropriate; Canetti's thesis is that human relations with nature
must have begun with mimetic contacts and competences that are difficult
to describe in the language of later historical periods. Because of the total
human involvement that seems to have been required, it would be misleading to stress only the role of the imagination. The affinity with Adorno's
conception of mimesis is beyond doubt, but differences should also be
noted. In particular, Adorno's understanding of mimesis was shaped by the
contrast with an idea of domination that Canetti must — although he never
made any explicit comments to that effect — have seen as over-rationalized.

The original communion through transformation is a precondition for
the slowly growing human mastery over nature. This is not simply a restate-
ment of the well-known fact that primitive hunters imitated their quarry to
very good effect, and thus developed a technique that became important for
all later forms of power. For Canetti, imitation is a controlled, external and
derivative mode of transformation; it is already adapted to an instrumental
role, but it presupposes a more elementary transformational dimension of
human nature. The same applies, in a more specific sense, to the transfer of
images and techniques from the context of domination over nature to the
level of social power, and vice versa: this ongoing interchange is part of a
more general movement between two domains of human life. Canetti is
more interested in the projection of natural or nature-related models into
the social world than in the opposite process (he makes no reference to
Lewis Mumford's analysis of the archaic "megamachine," made up of human
masses commanded by despotic rulers but structured in ways that anticipated
later technological progress). A brief comment on slavery at the end of the
chapter on transformation suggests a new approach to very basic structures
of social power. Canetti rejects the widespread notion — rooted in legal
formulations — that a slave can be defined as an object of possession: this
obscures the fundamental and anthropologically significant fact that slavery

is first of all an attempt to transform human beings into animals. The desire to achieve this goal should be recognized as a fundamental factor, operative across a wide range of historical situations. Here it might be objected that Canetti does not allow for multiple historical layers. His point may be valid for the most archaic aspect of slavery as an institution (and more pertinent than the interpretations that assume an indiscriminate objectification of human beings). But a closer look at the history of slavery, especially in the classical and more particularly the Roman world, suggests that a strategy of instrumental rationalization through more radical dehumanization was grafted onto the archaic infrastructure. This criticism is, however, not directed against Canetti's key point: the institution of slavery exemplifies an ambiguous relationship between power and transformation, inasmuch as its core structure makes use of the human ability to transform other humans, but in such a way that a coercive identity is perpetuated and autonomous transformations excluded.

The caste system can also be seen as an attempt to stabilize the conflictual relationship between power and transformation. It is, on the one hand a highly adaptable and integrative way of accommodating all kinds of sociocultural diversity, and as such (more specifically in its exemplary Indian version) it also provides a model for coping with more contingent intercultural encounters. With these aspects in mind, Canetti suggests that a closer look at its patterns would enable us to understand the sources of "all the different kinds of social transformation" (*CP*, 441). On the other hand, integration is achieved at the price of total immobility; in this regard, the caste regime is a "complete system of prohibitions" (*CP*, 441), but even from that point of view, the analysis of barriers can indirectly help to clarify the meaning of social ascent and ambition. Canetti notes that a transformational perspective has yet to be applied to the caste system. But his own main interest is not the study of large-scale institutional complexes and their functional mechanisms; rather, his focus is on condensed expressions and paradigmatic models of power. The idea of the *figure* is central to this line of thought.

Figures and Formations

A figure is a "final state of transformation" (*CP*, 432 — amended translation: the published English version refers to a "product" where Canetti speaks of an *Endzustand*), a fully matured and rounded result that bars the way to further transformations. But Canetti adds that the very process of transformation is the oldest figure (*CP*, 433). Both these descriptions can perhaps be summed up by saying that the most representative figures are those that come closest to capturing and at the same time immobilizing the intrinsic meaning of transformation. In view of what has been said about transformation as a link between humanity and nature, the genealogy of figures can begin with totemic fusions of human and animal features (sometimes, but less typically, amalgamations of human beings with plants or inanimate objects). But early historical religions, associated with visible power and emerging statehood, develop more elaborate ways of combining human and animal characteristics in a variety of divine figures. Ancient Egyptian religion is cited as the prime example (*CP*, 432). At this point, the analysis of figures becomes more explicitly concerned with power; in the institutionalized polytheisms of early civilizations the patterning of transformation intermingles with representations of power, and is by the same token involved in the construction of political order. From a comparative perspective, the "dual animal-human figures" (*CP*, 432) seem less important than Canetti's particular emphasis on them would suggest. Such images of divinity are, for example, much less characteristic of Mesopotamian religion than of the Egyptian pantheon. But this is not to say that the idea of figures as ways of aligning or identifying transformation with power is on the wrong track. It is — notwithstanding Canetti's distrust of concepts — an ingenious and instructive attempt to conceptualize the intermediate domain where transformation lends new meaning to power while power imposes a constraining meaning on transformation.

From this point of view, the most interesting figures are "the two best articulated forms of power known to the older civilizations" (*CP*, 441–42; this is a somewhat freewheeling translation: Canetti uses the term *Machthaber* and refers to the early history of humanity, not to civilizations), the shaman and the sacred king. Canetti's analysis of these opposite cases is highly suggestive, but very brief and inconclusive: they appear in a survey of prohibitions against transformation and are then set aside without any explicit connection to the subsequent reflections on aspects of power. If we want to take the argument further, we must begin with a recapitulation of the main contrasts. The shaman (prefigured by the less developed mythical figure of the trickster) is a "master transformer" and "the one to whom the largest number of transformations is open" (*CP*, 441 — Canetti's term is *Meistverwandler*); his ability to metamorphose into a wide variety of animals is matched by a capacity to move and act on different levels of cosmic reality. In this case, power seems to have been sublimated into the empowerment of transformation. Exceptional success in that regard sets the shaman apart from the common run of mankind, but does not — unless this figure is mixed with others — command obedience. The sacred king stands at the other end of the spectrum: he embodies static power par excellence. Canetti singles out the most extreme variant of sacred kingship, where the prohibition on transformation is so absolute that the incumbent must be destroyed when his dependence on the natural cycle of growth and decline becomes apparent. Here power moves as close as it can to a total suppression of transformation, but this results in exposure to periodic self-destruction. The sacred king stands outside and above the routines of social life, and his way of marking distance entails power over others — including the power to use, enact and limit transformation. Canetti claims that this image of a static center, exempt from the transformations that it imposes on others, is still reflected in modern conceptions of power, but he does not go on to track specific connections.

The two diametrically opposed ways of relating power to transformation exemplify key themes of Canetti's work. They can also serve to link his insights to other approaches. Both the sacred king and the shaman are presented as figures, and in that sense as enduring products of transformation, but from another angle, they function as foci and substrata for a new round of transformations. This claim is more easily substantiated in the case of sacred kingship: it has clearer institutional contours and has — on the basis of a much more conclusive historical record — been the subject of more extensive comparative studies than shamanism. The first point to note concerns its role in the most fundamental transformation of human societies. Following Gauchet's analysis, sacred kingship can be seen as a key factor in the primary process of state formation and in the concomitant mutation of sociocultural order. It shifts the center of religious life closer to the human world, but does so in a way that enhances the separation of power from society. In other words: the institution of sacred kingship is a transformative force of the first order. At the same time, Canetti's analysis of it as a figure remains valid in the sense that the fusion of sacred order and central power constitutes an eminently effective and durable stabilizing framework. But the ways of realizing this potential vary from one civilizational pattern to another, and the very counterweight to transformation thus becomes a starting point for further transformations. It may be useful to distinguish between sacred kingship, in the narrow sense of a direct divinization of the ruler, and sacral kingship as a broader category covering a whole spectrum of images and institutions that relate monocratic power to religious foundations. In the context of archaic civilizations, the former term is most obviously applicable to Egypt (the self-perpetuating sacred monarchy par excellence), whereas the latter covers the more fragmented and unstable Mesopotamian pattern: rulers of small states locked in permanent rivalry claimed the status of privileged servants or representatives of the gods, but no divinity in their own right. Both these traditions proved conducive to further changes, inside and outside their original orbits. As Jan Assmann has shown, the monotheistic turn taken in Ancient Israel — with the transfer of sovereignty to a creator god who was also a legislator — can be understood as a systematic rejection of the Egyptian model, articulated through a narrative of exodus from the Egyptian realm.[10] The monotheistic tradition thus begins with a transformative response to the archetypal case of sacred kingship. As for Mesopotamia, the idea of a universal empire grew out of never-ending struggles for hegemony and found a first mature regional expression in the Achaemenid Empire, before undergoing new changes in broader contexts. But apart from a brief attempt at the very outset, the imperial vision did not entail a direct deification of the ruler.

Other traditions transformed the idea and the institution of sacred kingship in different ways. The contrast between India and China has often been noted. In India, an early separation of priestly and royal authority had a decisive effect on the whole sociocultural order. Louis Dumont saw the relationship between brahmins and kings as a limited secularization of the political sphere and went on to link this thesis to a detailed interpretation of the caste system; other scholars have criticized his views, but the centrality of the separation as such is hardly contested. By contrast, the Chinese Empire perpetuated sacred kingship in a particularly elaborate form. The imperial institution survived into the twentieth century, and its posthumous presence is still noticeable. This does not mean that there were no cultural counterweights to the sacred ruler. Both the ideal of the sage and the more practical model of the scholar-statesman who could admonish an emperor without contesting the imperial institution played a balancing role.

Finally, the Greek case should at least be briefly mentioned. The unusually complete collapse of Mycenaean civilization put an end to a political order centered on sacred kingship (less well known than the Near Eastern models and apparently of a somewhat different type) and left behind what J.-P. Vernant calls a "crisis of sovereignty"; the Greek *polis,* with its radically new forms of political life and new directions of political reflection, emerged in this vacuum.[11]

The comparative history of sacred kingship and its variations is thus a master key to the cultural metamorphoses of power. More specifically, it highlights the role of the transformative imagination as a component of power structures. But the transformative potential of human nature also appears as a challenge and counterweight to the established forms of power. The figure of the shaman points in this direction. Here it is much more difficult to find a firm basis for comparative approaches; we must rest content with plausible analogies. The complex of phenomena commonly subsumed under the label of shamanism is most closely associated with archaic Inner Asian religions (it may be noted in passing that Canetti's particular interest in the Mongols — to which we will return — did not lead him to reflect on the shamanic background to their imperial religion). How far the concept can be generalized beyond this area is a matter of debate among historians of religion, but some suggestive parallels have been drawn. The most ambitious and erudite analyst of shamanism, Mircea Eliade, emphasized the specific features of the Inner Asian pattern, but also the points of contact with the religious imaginary of other traditions; his search for affinities with shamanism led to far-reaching cross-cultural conjectures (including those regarding the role and meaning of Apollo in Greek religion). There is no need to follow all the details of his argument; but it seems safe to assume that shamanism belongs to a broader context of more or less related religious phenomena. The most suggestive and far-reaching connection to explore is the affinity between shamanic journeys (as ways of communicating with other worlds) and the practices of divination. Research in the comparative history of religions has drawn attention to differences between cultural models of divination and to the lasting impact of these models on modes of thought (including the beginnings of philosophical traditions). In various archaic civilizations, techniques of divination became frameworks for rationalizing processes that in the long run contributed to the differentiation of cultural spheres and their autonomy with regard to the centers of power.[12] One of the most instructive cases is China, where a distinctive "divinatory imaginary" was at first closely associated with (and subordinated to) an early paradigm of sacred kingship, but later involved in the genesis of more detached intellectual currents (perhaps most visibly in the development of the Taoist tradition and its images of sagehood beyond the reach of power).[13] Although the relative importance of a shamanic substratum in ancient Chinese culture is a matter of debate and speculation, the presence of a broader constellation of related meanings is well attested.

From Transformation to Tyranny

The comparison of shamanism and sacred kingship can thus be read as a key to the cultural history of power, and to its unending interplay with the transformative imagination. The force that lends authoritative and formative meaning to power is also active on the other side: it is a permanent source of efforts to weaken the grip of power or minimize its destructive potential. To put it in more extreme terms, transformation is the common ground of despotism and subversion. It is not being suggested that shamanism is the direct or sole ancestor of cultural challenges to power; but analyses of the shamanic phenomenon have traced connections with religious and cultural sources of creative innovation. To note this potential range of Canetti's reflections — and to stress its importance for a more theoretical use of his insights — is not to criticize him for failing to take that direction. For him, that would have meant switching to an altogether new genre. In the context of his self-defined and uniquely unorthodox project, the figures of the shaman and the sacred king are not so much starting points for comparative history as archaic — and therefore primary — versions of contrasting human archetypes (or, to use a more phenomenological language, modes of being in the world). They are, in other words, alternative images of the human condition, and Canetti uses them as smaller-scale models of more extreme phenomena that he then goes on to describe in broader perspective. In his own environment the shaman is an exceptional figure, but he exemplifies the transformative abilities and dispositions that were presumably more widely diffused at an earlier stage of human history. He is thus a privileged heir to the otherwise half-lost world that Canetti was trying to re-imagine through descriptions of the Bushmen and their relationship to nature. By contrast, the sacred king is portrayed as a precursor of modern figures, and with implicit reference to Canetti's diagnoses of paranoia and dictatorship. The most extreme experiences of that kind belong to the twentieth century.

At first sight, then, the two figures point in opposite directions: back to a pristine state of transformation untroubled by power, and forwards to a modern image of power in complete control of transformation. Yet on closer examination Canetti's polarizing vision of the human condition proves irreducible to the contrast between primitive and modern. A return to the oldest accessible sources may be essential to our understanding of transformation, but so is the possession or re-appropriation of works created at crucial junctures and inspired by exceptional insight. Canetti's references to the *Epic of Gilgamesh* and to Ovid's *Metamorphoses* — mentioned above — should be recalled in this context. The story of Gilgamesh sums up a "great transforma-tion" — commonly known as the rise of civilization — with particular empha-sis on aspects and dimensions beyond the pursuit of power. Transformative experiences are recorded in a narrative that throws new light on the funda-mentals and the inbuilt enigmas of the human condition. But the case of Ovid's *Metamorphoses* is even more revealing, and Canetti's most extensive comment on the subject (*PM*, 349–50) is worth recapitulating in detail. Transformation was the very medium of the mythopoeic imagination, but by making it central to his poetic narrative, Ovid gave it a stronger meaning and brought the essentials of myth (*das Eigentlichste des Mythus*) to new and lasting prominence. He thus enriched cultural memory and transmitted to the later Christian world a whole imaginary (to use Castoriadis's term) that would always coexist uneasily with its dominant beliefs. For Canetti, Ovid's achieve-ment was significant enough to mark him as the founding father of a perpetual modernity. On another level, this assessment of the *Metamorphoses* can be read as a distinctive account of the classical legacy and its cultural impact. A brief reference to the cult of beauty as a reflection (*Abglanz*) of polytheism (*PM*, 281) suggests some ramifications of this view.

There is, however, another side to the Ovidian moment. Canetti's inter-pretation must be understood in light of his comments on the Romans regarding their power-obsessed mentality and their disastrous influence on the European political imagination. Ovid was a contemporary, a favorite, and finally a victim of the most effective and innovative empire-builder among Roman rulers, and in a sense, the re-created poetic universe of the *Metamor-phoses* represents a more enduring answer to the new order that Augustus imposed on the Mediterranean world. Although Canetti does not mention Augustus, it is tempting to reflect on the relationship between the founding emperor and the exiled poet whose work survived the empire: it may be seen as another variant of the constellation first exemplified by the sacred king and the shaman.

In short, the history of transformation — and of its interplay with power — has its cultural landmarks. Similarly, modern experiences of power at its most absolute and excessive can be understood in light of cultural models and historical traditions rather than as purely self-contained developments. Although Canetti insists that barbarism has never been more triumphant than in the contemporary world, and that humanity must be sought in the past (*NH*, 179), he also draws on past examples of power unleashed and uses them as keys to present phenomena of the same kind. The idea that modernity can only be understood through confrontation with something else is thus reaffirmed in a crucial context. In more specific terms, Canetti singled out Islamic rulers as classic representatives of the enemy whom he wanted to combat and destroy (*PM*, 217). His interpretation of Islam stresses the uniquely close but at the same time conflictual symbiosis of religion and power. The first thing to note is the "nakedness of domination" (*PM*, 217) in Islamic civilization, all the more striking because everything else is disguised and transfigured by the law. But naked power also relies on religious justification. The ruler's obedience to God translates into divine license for the arbitrary exercise of power. Canetti refers to "God as a murderer, who decides every single death and ensures that the sentence is carried out," and "the ruler who emulates God in the most naïve fashion" (*PM*, 217). This complicity of divine and human despotism is the culminating outcome of a logic already at work in Jewish monotheism. In the Islamic version, the power presented as obedience to an exclusive god is by the same token geared to universal rule over human beings; it is therefore most at home in large cosmopolitan cities. Finally, Canetti notes that the very constitutive extremism of Islamic power makes it permanently vulnerable to religious protest, but opposition is invariably channeled into struggles for power.

Canetti's reflections on Islam lead to an interesting account of its origins. Muhammad appears as the first prophet who seized power: he identified belief with obedience and envisaged the day of judgment as the most extreme and concentrated expression of domination (*PM*, 155). This view of the founder is not far removed from some traditional Western perceptions. But the interpretation of his political strategy is more original. His aim was, as Canetti sees it, to replace the oligarchy of the Kuraishites with a tyranny, and the decisive step was the building of a rival proto-state in Medina. The reference to an established oligarchy shows that "tyranny" is not used here as a purely rhetorical term: the historical analogy with the paradigmatic Greek case is unmistakable. Tyranny in the classical sense grew out of the conflicts and crises that accompanied the formation of the Greek *polis*. A structurally similar project that could mobilize the religious resources of monotheism was bound to develop in different ways. Although Canetti does not elaborate, his suggestions are clearly compatible with the most recent trends of scholarly debate. A strong case has been made for interpreting the rise of Islam and the beginnings of Islamic expansion as integral to the process of state formation on the Arabian periphery of the Near East; the long-term dynamics of internal power structures took a new turn under the impact of rivalry between two regional empires (Late Roman and Sassanian), and rapid conquest became possible when the struggle for hegemony had exhausted both imperial centers.[14] When an adaptive reinter-pretation of monotheism was grafted onto a political strategy tailored to this new constellation, the region was ripe for an imperial renewal that changed the course of world history.

For Canetti, the monotheistic fusion of belief and power prefigures a trend that found its most extreme expression in the totalitarian quest for unity of the ruled through identification with a unique ruler. Islam is, in this regard as in many others, the consummate form of monotheism. But it is not the only precedent that Canetti invokes to clarify the contemporary history of power. His particular interest in the Mongols, and in the record of their rise to imperial power in the *Secret History of the Mongols,* has to do with the elementary and paradigmatic character of this episode: the *Secret History* alone would suffice to reveal the fundamental laws of power (*PM*, 214), and in that respect, it is comparable to the Bible, but the latter mixes visions of power with other themes that have often overshadowed them. Canetti does not discuss the religion of the Mongols. The focus is, rather, on Genghis Khan's extreme version of despotic power, reminiscent of the claims made elsewhere on behalf of an exclusive god, although the beliefs behind it were much more adaptable (and in the end open to conversion) than monotheis-tic religions. The *Secret History* is the inside story of the most uninterrupt-edly successful pursuit of power within a single life span. Analogies with Schreber and Hitler suggest that the "laws of power" may operate in simi-larly extreme ways in other contexts, even if modalities and results vary widely. The Mongol experience is, however, particularly noteworthy for another reason: this uniquely expansionistic form of power "emerged among people for whom *money* could not mean anything. It became visible through the movements of horses and arrows. It came from an early world of hunters and robbers, and it conquered the rest of the world" (*PM*, 214). It repre-sents, in other words, a bridge between different historical universes, and a reminder of omnipresent but not always manifest essentials of power. From that point of view, the story of the Mongol Empire complements the much longer and more variegated record of Islamic rulers. One might therefore expect the conquerors and empires that drew on both sources — beginning with Tamerlane — to figure more prominently in Canetti's historical phe-nomenology of power. But he did not pursue the matter further. His most detailed portrait of an Islamic ruler is the section on Muhammad Tughlak, sultan of Delhi (*CP*, 493–505); because of the Turkish origins of the Tugh-lak dynasty, we can assume that an Inner Asian background counted for something, but it is more difficult to detect any specific Mongol connection of the kind evident in Tamerlane and his heirs.

The Long March through Myths and Religions

As we have seen, Canetti's bipolar anthropology — centered on the antagonistic interdependence of power and transformation, and symbolized by the twin figures of the sacred king and the shaman — is too complex to be understood as a defense of the archaic against the modern. There is no primordial form of social life without active pursuit of power, and no linear dynamic of power encroaching upon the domain of transformation. On the other hand, and notwithstanding these basic qualifications, there is no denying the particular importance of archaic sources for Canetti's attempt to rehabilitate the transformational side of human nature against the more familiar but not *ipso facto* better understood imagery of power. He often confesses to a hubristic and insatiable desire to know all myths of all peoples; this "search for all the old gods" (*NH,* 30) was a conscious effort to atone for the exclusivism of his Jewish ancestors. The particular importance of primitive myths is obvious. They reveal the range of human diversity more effectively than the culturally circumscribed myths integrated into the European tradition, and they provide some support for the conjecture that our understanding of transformation could be improved through closer study of early beginnings (even if there is no suggestion of a state of complete immunity to power). Canetti's interest in primitive cultures led him to see the recently established discipline of anthropology as a superior version of traditional humanism. His statements to that effect are strikingly reminiscent of those found in Lévi-Strauss's work, and for both thinkers (notwithstanding Lévi-Strauss's highly technical analyses of primitive institutions), the imaginary universe of myths is ultimately more important for the anthropological project than is the institutional background. But we can safely rule out any direct influence.

Primitive myths are doubly relevant to the question of transformation: they tell stories about transformations, and they exemplify the human ability to create, inhabit, and articulate different worlds. Canetti is fully conscious of the difficulties inherent in his attempt to understand them: "description is further removed from myth than anything else, and that is perhaps why I am ashamed of it" (*NH,* 38). But empathic descriptions of the kind illustrated by *Crowds and Power* (as well as some of his other writings) are also to be read as exercises in transformation. The writer strives to re-imagine the object of description from within, even when the ultimate intention is to unmask it and weaken its hold on the human imagination (in that sense, Canetti speaks of "becoming a Mongol" during his immersion in the *Secret History)*. The reader is thus, once again, reminded of the vast domain behind the "closed door" (*PM,* 249) to a better understanding of transformation. For present purposes, however, our main concern is the particular insight to be achieved through primitive myths. It seems logical to assume that this has to do with a broader grasp of the religious imagination and its products. Canetti confesses to a passion for "religions and myths" (*NH,* 19). But if we try to reconstruct his understanding of religion, the most suggestive statements seem to point in different directions. He professes allegiance to many religions (once again, with an explicit and polemical reference to his Jewish heritage), and expects them to coalesce — in due course — into a single one (*PM,* 10). On the other hand, the landing on the moon destroys his previously most secure religious faith (*NH,* 187; we can only surmise that he is alluding to a belief in an immutably earthbound destiny of humanity). He singles out the simplicity of all religions as a reason why he is attracted to them (*NH,* 172), but he also sees it as a weakness of all religions that they always speak of the same things, and this may explain why "living spirits like Stendhal" (one of his idols) rejected them (*NH,* 39). Religions that do not reflect an underlying fear are dismissed as shallow (*NH,* 7), but at the same time we can see unmistakable signs of preference for religions that show sensitivity to the poetic potential of transformation. (This is perhaps most evident in his comments on the "colorful character" of Buddhism, *NH,* 188.)

Other examples of ambiguity could be added to this list. It would be inappropriate to criticize Canetti for lack of conceptual precision: his shifting perspectives on the human nature and history of religions reflect a more fundamental indeterminacy of his main theme. As we have seen, he insists on the need for further efforts to understand transformation and on the inadequacy of traditional philosophical approaches. If this decisive but neglected dimension of human nature is to be given its due, a whole new language must be created; the first step is to perceive the field of transformations in all its protean variety, without concessions to the unifying — and *eo ipso* simplifying — logic that aligns thought with power. The multiple and divergent meanings of transformation reappear in more specific contexts, not least in those of the myths and religions that Canetti set out to explore. The phenomenon — and the problem — of belief is central to his reflections and indicative of the difficulties arising when comparative approaches to religion move onto new ground. His particular concern with this issue is evident in various statements throughout his work. In 1944, he refers to the "question of belief" as the most momentous and unsettling of all problems encountered by human beings (*PM*, 77). Twenty years later, he admits to a permanent obsession with the same question and to the hope that his efforts will bring him closer to understanding the nature of belief (*NH*, 72). This aim is integral to his study of myths: he wants to know them "as if he had believed in them" (*PM*, 95). The same reason explains "a growing passion for all sects, whatever their religious background" (*PM*, 77). Sects are, by definition, prone to translate minor variations of content into rival beliefs and religious conflicts, and this very characteristic might make their historical record particularly revealing as to the nature of belief. But Canetti adds that the study of sects also helps him to liberate himself from attachment to any belief. Both understanding and detachment can thus benefit from closer study of diverse beliefs in general and sectarian distinctions in particular.

The question of belief — broadly understood — is directly related to Canetti's idea of transformation. The variety of beliefs, in the sense of commitments to particular ideas, traditions and identities, and to ways of building separate worlds around them, is the most emphatic expression of human mutability. That applies most obviously to religious systems of belief and their cultural universes. But they also exemplify another side of the relationship between belief and transformation. The constitution — and more or less thoroughgoing closure — of worlds based on beliefs sets limits to transformation and blocks insight into its more radical implications. The classic works that transcend these limits and grasp transformation at a deeper level are few and far between; they represent privileged moments in cultural history.

Canetti's general reflections on myth, religion, and belief raise more questions than they answer. It remains to be seen whether specific views on the history of religions add up to a more conclusive picture. Two approaches, outlined in brief but suggestive comments and implicit in various observations elsewhere in Canetti's writings, seem particularly promising. On the one hand, the history of religions — culminating in the world religions — appears as a progressive loss of meaning, explicitly comparable to the mathematization of scientific knowledge and reminiscent of the "emptying-out process" (*Entleerungsprozess*) associated with philosophy (*NH*, 40–41). To clarify how religions can — despite the development of complex interpretive frameworks — contribute to the loss of meaning, Canetti's specific viewpoint must be taken into account. The starting point is the pre-existence of myths — now clearly distinguished from religions — and their close connection with the naming of things: "all myths depend on the name" (*NH*, 40). For Canetti, names are "the most mysterious of all words," and a better understanding of their meaning might improve the self-knowledge of humanity as much as the deciphering of archaic writing systems has improved our knowledge of forgotten cultures. If names are of particular importance for the mythopoeic imagination, that can only be due to their role as individual foci of meaning, with open horizons of connotation and narrative elaboration. Within the increasingly centered and structured frameworks of institutionalized religions, they lose this autonomy. As Canetti puts it, they now serve to bind rather than to release; this reflects the more general alignment with and affirmation of power that become manifest in the monotheistic religions.

The other perspective goes beyond the conventional history of religions: it has to do with the elementary forms of secular religion (Canetti never uses that term, but it seems adequate; other analysts have used it in the same context). Here the starting point is a critique of the Enlightenment; more specifically of its failure to tackle the "most absurd" of all religions, the religion of power (*PM*, 41). Those who denounced obsolete forms of belief left this tradition unchallenged and even aided its survival in a modern setting. Canetti distinguishes two post-Enlightenment ways of practicing the religion of power. It can be continued in the traditional fashion, without inventive rhetoric but with unbroken links to classical models. (As we have seen, the Romans figure most prominently among the latter.) For Canetti, this alternative is likely to prove more dangerous in the long run. The other, more innovative and aggressive, "declared itself publicly as a religion" and aspired to replace the "dying religions of love." Its credo was: "God is power, and whoever can is his prophet" (*PM*, 41). This was written in 1943, when the most extreme version of the second type was on the defensive after unprecedentedly rapid success in the first round. Nazism has invariably been singled out as a prime example by analysts of secular religions. It may be less obvious why this concept should apply to the traditional religion of power as described by Canetti. A plausible reason can perhaps be found in the relationship between power, death, and survival: if the historical structures of power cannot be understood without reference to the efforts of individuals to overcome death (*PM*, 364), this connection can also be seen as a link to the religious imagination. The quest for surrogate immortality through power is an attempt to transfigure the human condition, and as such, it belongs — in a paradoxical and perverse way — to the domain of transformation.

Religious Dimensions of Power

If there is, in this fundamental sense, a religious side to the pursuit of power, we can take the argument further and explore ways of combining the two perspectives mentioned above. The first point to be noted is an underlying complicity between the primary religion of power and the more complex products of the religious imagination. Canetti's reflections on the major religions of world history converge in one central and decisive objection: in one way or another, they all evade the challenge of death. This is not to suggest that differences between them are irrelevant. Buddhism is unique in that it tries to neutralize death through a negation of life, but does so in a subtle way that leaves considerable scope for sensitivity to transformations. There may be one genuine exception to the general rule: for Canetti, Taoism is "the religion of poets, even when they do not know it" (*PM*, 334), because of its this-worldly vision of immortality and its straightforward emphasis on transformation. But Taoism never became a world religion, and even within the Chinese world it was confined to a subordinate position. The most successful world religions — the two monotheistic ones, both based on adapted versions of a Jewish invention — are also most conducive to phantasms of power and most concerned with illusory compensations for death.

Monotheism maximizes the original complicity of religion and power. It develops images of absolute and concentrated power on a cosmic scale; they can inspire more or less overt aspirations to godlike authority on the part of human rulers, but they can also mutate into post-traditional visions of the kind familiar from twentieth-century experiences with totalitarianism. Canetti's reflections on the totalitarian phenomenon, especially his brilliant essay on Hitler (*GW*, 171–99), take a distinctive turn and are in some ways closer to current views — those of authors writing after the collapse of the major totalitarian regimes — than to the contemporary observers of ascendant totalitarianism. The pioneering analysts who saw the totalitarian project as an acute threat were also inclined to regard it as a noticeable shift in the other direction: totalitarianism is now more frequently subsumed under the general concept of tyranny, and arguments about its radical novelty are dismissed as exaggerations of the particular twentieth-century aspects of its conflict with liberalism.[15] There is no doubt where Canetti stands in this controversy. His reflections on power lead to a radical diagnosis and critique of tyranny. But as he sees it, there are two sides to this phenomenon. On the one hand, it exemplifies elementary and universal laws of power; in that sense, a meta-historical definition of tyranny is justified. On the other hand, its general features are magnified and radicalized by monotheism, first through direct and later through indirect influences. Monotheism must, in turn, be understood as the outcome of a long history revolving around the ambiguous relationship between religion and transformation. The triumphant world religions are those that have most effectively absorbed, instrumentalized and perverted the transformational potential of human nature.

Canetti's idea of transformation links the relationship between religion and power to a broader cultural context. Further discussion of contrasts and parallels with more conventional interpretations of culture is beyond the scope of this book. But to conclude, we must return to a question posed at the beginning of this argument: has the analysis of transformation and its religious ramifications thrown any light on the main point at issue in Canetti's critique of Hobbes? Canetti noted Hobbes's failure to grasp the composite character of self-interest (the common denominator of economic and political man); although this objection touches upon the most fundamental problems of theorizing power, he never took it up again. In that sense, he failed to spell out his reasons for proposing an alternative view of power, and the present interpretation does not claim to provide the answer that he left pending. It may, however, be suggested that some indications of the direction to take are implicit in the above discussion. Unifying images or conceptions of power are — as Canetti sees it — imposed on a more heterogeneous substratum; they are, in other words, the results of transformational processes that take a paradoxically self-negating turn. This idea is developed with particular reference to the practices and phantasms of tyrannical rulers. But there are occasional allusions to the more elementary level where Hobbes located the mainsprings of self-interest. One of the most instructive formulations comes at the end of Canetti's analysis of Schreber's memoir: "It is difficult to resist the suspicion that behind paranoia, as behind all power, lies the same profound urge: the desire to get other men out of the way so as to be the only one: or, in the milder, and indeed often admitted form, to get others to help him *become* the only one" (*CP*, 537). The totalitarian extreme of tyranny is thus put in a perspective that suggests affinities with radical individualism (of the instrumental or strategic kind that the sociological classics distinguished from a more universalistic one). Although Hobbes is not mentioned, the whole statement can be read as a variation on his central theme: the profit-seeking private citizen and the wise ruler are replaced by the anomic individual and the paranoid tyrant. Both of them are products of a history that has channeled the transformational potential of human nature into leveling and impoverishing forms. It is tempting to draw a parallel with Hannah Arendt's interpretation of Hobbes. In both cases, a more critical reading of *Leviathan* goes beyond the model of a transitional compromise between liberalism and absolutism; the alternative hypothesis is that the anthropological infrastructure of liberalism — defined in terms of modern ways to pursue wealth and power — might be inherently and permanently vulnerable to totalitarian twists. Canetti's general view of the modern world was clearly compatible with that line of thought; but his anthropological reflections were too focused on remote origins and too resistant to conceptual elaboration for the agreement to become more explicit.

Notes

Introduction

[1] In keeping with the primary aim of the present study — to open up Canetti's work to the wider context of social theory — the comparative focus of the discussion of *Auto da Fé* in chapter one is intended to complement rather than engage with the existing literature on the novel. Some points of contact with other interpretations are indicated in the notes.

[2] See in particular the articles by Gerhard Neumann, "Widerrufe des Sündenfalls" in *Hüter der Verwandlung* (Munich: Hanser, 1985); Jürgen Söring, "Die Literatur als Provinz des Menschen," *Deutsche Vierteljahrsschrift für Literaturwissenschaft* 60 (1986); Peter von Matt, "Der phantastische Aphorismus bei Elias Canetti," in Adrian Stevens and Fred Wagner, eds., *Elias Canetti: Londoner Symposium* (Stuttgart: Heinz, 1991); and the monographs by Susanne Engelmann, *Babel — Bibel — Bibliothek: Canettis Aphorismen zur Sprache* (Würzburg: Könighausen & Neumann, 1997) and Eric Leroy du Cardonnoy, *Les Réflexions d'Elias Canetti: une esthétique de la discontinuité* (Bern: Lang, 1997).

[3] The articles by Axel Honneth, "The Perpetuation of the State of Nature," *Thesis Eleven* 45 (1996), and by Iring Fetscher, "*Masse und Macht* und die Erklärung totalitärer Gesellschaften," in John Pattillo-Hess, ed., *Verwandlungsverbote und Befreiungsversuche in Canettis Masse und Macht* (Vienna, Löcker, 1991) are indicative of the reserve with which social scientists continue to regard *Crowds and Power*. The chief exception in this history of non-reception is J. S. McClelland, *The Crowd and the Mob from Plato to Canetti* (London: Unwin Hyman, 1989). More recently Michael Mack, *Anthropology as Memory: Elias Canetti's and Franz Baermann Steiner's Responses to the Shoah* (Tübingen: Niemayer, 2001) seeks to reconstruct the intellectual and historical context for *Crowds and Power* with particular reference to French and British anthropology. See also Ritchie Robertson, "Canetti as Anthropologist," in Adrian Stevens and Fred Wagner, eds., *Elias Canetti: Londoner Symposium* (Stuttgart: Heinz, 1991), 132–45.

[4] We are referring to the conference volumes edited by John Pattillo-Hess, and by Penka Angelova (see bibliography). Papers of particular relevance are indicated in the notes to the individual chapters. The collection of essays edited by Michael Krüger, *Einladung zur Verwandlung* (Munich: Hanser, 1995) is primarily of interest as a document of the reception of *Crowds and Power*.

[5] Cardonnoy's *Les Réflexions d'Elias Canetti* provides the best account of Canetti's anti-systematic strategies in terms of an aesthetics of discontinuity that sets out to challenge Western ideas of linearity, causality, closure, and teleology.

Chapter 1

[1] See the section "July 15" in Part Three of Elias Canetti, *Torch in My Ear* (New York: Farrar, Straus and Giroux, 1986); Gerald Stieg, *Frucht des Feuers: Canetti, Doderer, Kraus und der Justizpalastbrand* (Vienna: Edition Falter im Österreichischen Bundesverlag, 1990).

[2] On Canetti and Lukács see David Roberts, "Die Blendung der gesamten Romanliteratur: Bemerkungen zu Canettis paradoxer Romanpoetik," in Gerhard Neumann, ed., *Canetti als Leser* (Freiburg: Rombach, 1996), 49–58.

[3] Herbert Schnädelbach, *Philosophie in Deutschland 1831–1933* (Frankfurt: Suhrkamp, 1994), 176.

[4] Georg Simmel, "The Tragedy of Culture," in David Frisby and Mike Featherstone, eds., *Simmel on Culture: Selected Writings* (London: Sage, 1997); Georg Lukács, *History and Class Consciousness,* trans. Rodney Livingstone (London: Merlin Press, 1971 [1923]); Walter Benjamin, *The Origin of German Tragic Drama,* trans. John Osborne (London: NLB, 1977 [1928]); Ludwig Klages, *Der Geist als Widersacher der Seele* 3 vols. (Leipzig: Barth, 1929–1933).

[5] See Helmut König, *Zivilisation und Leidenschaften. Die Masse im bürgerlichen Zeitalter* (Reinbek bei Hamburg: Rowohlt, 1992).

[6] Georges Sorel, *Reflections on Violence* (New York: Collier Books, 1961[1908]); Norbert Elias, *The Civilizing Process: Sociogenetic and Psychogenetic Investigations* (Oxford: Blackwell, 2000 [1939]).

[7] See Zeev Sternhell with Mario Sznajder and Maria Ashari, *The Birth of Fascist Ideology: From Cultural Rebellion to Political Revolt,* trans. David Maisel (Princeton, NJ: Princeton UP, 1994) and Carl Schorske, "Politics in a New Key," in Schorske, *Fin-de-Siècle Vienna: Politics and Culture* (New York: Knopf, 1980). For the wider Viennese cultural and social background, including anti-Semitism, see Maurice Godé, Ingrid Haag, and Jacques Le Rider, eds., "Wien-Berlin: Deux sites de la modernité," in *Cahiers d'Études Germaniques* 24 (1993) and Jacques Le Rider, *Modernity and Crises of Identity: Culture and Society in Fin-de-Siècle Vienna,* trans. Rosemary Morris (Cambridge: Polity Press, 1993).

[8] Sternhell, *The Birth of Fascist Ideology,* 254.

[9] Cf. Robert Elbaz and Leah Hadomi, *Elias Canetti or the Failing of the Novel* (New York: Lang, 1995): the novel "problematizes the very relationship between text and context, the word and the world, story and history, signifier and signified. What is at stake here is the very possibility of the novel and, by extension, of the Text in general . . . to extract a minimal signification from the historical phenomena it

purports to metaphorize" (5). See also William Collins Donahue, *End of Modernism: Elias Canetti's Auto-da-Fe* (Chapel Hill, NC: U of North Carolina P, 2001).

[10] Cornelius Castoriadis, *The Imaginary Institution of Society,* trans. Kathleen Blemey (Cambridge: Polity Press, 1987), 344.

[11] Castoriadis, *The Imaginary Institution,* 351.

[12] Georg Lukács, *History and Class Consciousness: Studies in Marxist Dialectics,* trans. Rodney Livingstone (London: Merlin Press, 1971), 194.

[13] See Elias Canetti, "Inflation and the Crowd," in *Crowds and Power,* trans. Carol Stewart (Harmondsworth, England: Penguin, 1973 [1962]), 214–20.

[14] Norbert Elias, *The Society of Individuals,* ed. Michael Schröter and trans. Edmund Jephcott (Oxford: Blackwell, 1991).

[15] Canetti, "Das erste Buch," in Herbert Göpfert, ed., *Canetti lesen* (Munich: Hanser, 1975), 131.

[16] See Gerard Stieg, "Canetti und die Psychoanalyse: Das Unbehagen in der Kultur und Die Blendung," in Adrian Stevens and Fred Wagner, eds., *Elias Canetti: Londoner Symposium* (Stuttgart: Heinz, 1991), 59–74 and Lothar Hennighaus, *Tod und Verwandlung: Elias Canettis poetische Anthropologie aus der Kritik der Psychoanalyse* (Frankfurt: Lang, 1984).

[17] Norbert Elias, *Über den Prozess der Zivilisation: Soziogenetische und psychogenetische Untersuchungen,* vol. 1 (Frankfurt: Suhrkamp, 1977), lxiv. Quotations in the text are from this edition.

[18] Hermann Hesse, *Steppenwolf,* trans. Basil Creighton (New York: Holt, Rinehart and Winston, n.d.), 55–56.

[19] Helmut König, *Zivilisation und Leidenschaften: Die Masse im bürgerlichen Zeitalter,* 143–57.

[20] See the chapter "Massendiskurs" in König, *Zivilisation und Leidenschaften.*

[21] See Michael Rohrwasser, "Elias Canettis Auseinandersetzung mit der Psychoanalyse in seinem Roman Die Blendung," *Convivium* 2000: 43–64.

[22] Castoriadis, *The Imaginary Institution,* 302.

[23] Castoriadis, *The Imaginary Institution,* 302.

[24] The figure of Fischerle epitomizes the problem of Jewish identity and anti-Semitism. See Nicola Riedner, *Canettis Fischerle: Eine Figur zwischen Masse, Macht und Blendung* (Würzburg: Königshausen & Neumann, 1994).

[25] Werner Koch, ed., *Selbstanzeige: Schriftsteller im Gespräch* (Frankfurt: Fischer, 1971), 34. See also Sigmund Freud, "Group Psychology and the Analysis of the Ego," in *The Penguin Freud Library* XII (London, Penguin, 1991): 176.

[26] Castoriadis, *The Imaginary Institution,* 300.

[27] See Elfriede Pöder, "Spurensicherung: Otto Weininger in der Blendung," in Friedrich Aspetsberger and Gerard Stieg, eds., *Blendung als Lebensform: Elias Canetti*

(Königstein: Athenäum, 1985), 57–72. On Weininger see also Jacques Le Rider, *Modernity and Crises of Identity.*

[28] Ernst Jünger, *Der Arbeiter* (Stuttgart: Klett, 1981), 243–45.

[29] Simmel regards the conflict between life and form as the "deepest internal contradiction of the spirit" and argues that the present age is distinguished by the assault of life against form as such arising from the perception of cultural exhaustion. Georg Simmel, *The Conflict of Form and Other Essays,* trans. K. Peter Etzkorn (New York: Teachers College Press, 1968).

[30] Ernst Cassirer, *The Philosophy of Symbolic Forms,* vol. 1: *Language,* trans. Ralph Manheim (New Haven: Yale UP, 1955), 111–14.

[31] Hans Blumenberg, "Ernst Cassirers gedenkend," in Blumenberg, *Wirklichkeiten in denen wir leben* (Stuttgart: Reclam, 1981), 167.

[32] Ernst Cassirer, *The Philosophy of Symbolic Forms,* Vol. 2: *Mythical Thought,* trans. Ralph Manheim (New Haven: Yale UP, 1955), 46. Quotations in the text are taken from this edition. See also the section "Phänomenologie des mythischen Denkens bei Cassirer und Canetti: Das mythopoetische Konzept," in Peter Zepp, *Privatmythos und Wahn: Das mythopoetische Konzept im Werk Elias Canettis* (Frankfurt: Lang, 1990), 183–204.

[33] Canetti, *Die Provinz des Menschen: Aufzeichnungen 1942–1972* (Munich: Hanser, 1973), 24.

[34] Canetti, "Das erste Buch," 131–32.

Chapter 2

[1] Saul Bellow, *Herzog* (Harmondsworth, England: Penguin, 1965), 83, 323.

[2] Serge Moscovici, *The Age of the Crowd* (Cambridge: Cambridge UP, 1985), 111. But see also his contribution, "Social Collectivities," in *Essays in Honour of Elias Canetti* (London: Andre Deutsch, 1987), 42–59.

[3] Moscovici, "The Discovery of the Masses" in Carol Graumann and S. Moscovici, eds., *Changing Conceptions of Crowd Mind and Behaviour* (New York/Berlin: Springer, 1986), 5–26.

[4] Moscovici, *The Age of the Crowd,* 241.

[5] Moscovici, *The Age of the Crowd,* 287.

[6] Sigmund Freud, "Group Psychology and the Analysis of the Ego" in *The Penguin Freud Library XII* (London: Penguin, 1991), 153. In the English translation "group" is used throughout for Freud's "Masse," McDougall's "group," and Le Bon's "foule."

[7] Unlike the theories of Adorno and Arendt, the parallels and contrasts between Canetti's *Crowds and Power* and Hermann Broch's theory of crowd madness and crowd hysteria as a contribution to a psychology of politics have been the subject of a number of studies: Sigrid Schmid-Bortenschlager, "Der Einzelne und seine Masse.

Massentheorie und Literaturkonzeption bei Elias Canetti und Hermann Broch," in Kurt Bartsch and Gerhard Melzer, eds., *Experte der Macht: Elias Canetti* (Graz: Droschl, 1985), 116–32; N. S. Zopotoczky, "Canettis Massentheorie zwischen Adler und Broch," in John Pattillo-Hess, ed., *Canettis Masse und Macht oder Die Aufgabe des gegenwärtigen Denkens* (Vienna: Bundesverlag, 1988), 120–31; and Robert Weigel, "Elias Canettis Masse und Macht und Hermann Brochs Massenwahntheorie: Berührungspunkte und Unterschiede," in Joseph P. Strelka and Zsuzsa Szell, eds., *Ist die Wahrheit ein Meer von Grashalmen?* (Bern: Lang, 1993), 121–45.

[8] See the contrary argument in Johann P. Arnason, "The Dialectic of Enlightenment and the Post-Functionalist Theory of Society," *Thesis Eleven* 13 (1986): 77–93.

[9] Sigmund Freud, "The Future of an Illusion," *The Penguin Freud Library XII,* 194.

[10] Arnason, "The Dialectic of Enlightenment," 84.

[11] Sigmund Freud, "Civilization and its Discontents," *The Penguin Freud Library XII,* 313.

[12] Moscovici, "The Discovery of the Masses," 20.

[13] The influence of crowd theory on Freud's theory of the unconscious appears clearly in the following observation: "Our mind . . . is rather to be compared with a modern state in which a mob, eager for enjoyment and destruction, has to be held down by a prudent superior class." (Freud, "My Contact with Josef Popper Lynkeus" in Freud, *Standard Edition* 22 [London: Hogarth Press, n.d.]).

[14] Cf. David Roberts, "The Sense of an Ending: Apocalyptic Perspectives in the 20th Century German Novel," *Orbis Litterarum* 32 (1977): 140–58 for an analysis of *Auto da Fé* in the context of the 1920s. See also D. Roberts, *Kopf und Welt: Canettis Roman Die Blendung* (Munich: Hanser, 1975).

[15] Cf. Freud's comments on the triumph of survival, which apply not only towards the slain enemy but also towards loved ones, in "Thoughts for the Times on War and Death," *Penguin Freud Library XII,* 61–89.

[16] See Marcel Gauchet, *The Disenchantment of the World: A Political History of Religion,* trans. Oscar Burge (Princeton, NJ: Princeton UP, 1997).

[17] Arnold Toynbee stresses the monstrous birth of the power of the tyrant as the consequence of the "eruption of a Modern Western secular civilization out of the Medieval Western Respublica Christiana" in *A Study of History: Abridgement of Volumes VII–X* by D. C. Somervell (Oxford: Oxford UP, 1957), 112; Lewis Namier stresses the rise of the mass: "The mass is the refuge of the uprooted individual and the disintegration of spiritual values is as potent a process as the splitting of the atom: it releases demonic forces which burst all dams." (*Vanished Supremacies: Essays on European History 1812–1918* [Harmondsworth, England: Penguin, 1962], 53).

[18] Marc Richir, *Du sublime en politique* (Paris: Payot, 1991), 68.

[19] See Canetti's illuminating observations on Hitler's true crowd, the crowds of the dead, in his essay on Albert Speer's *Memoirs* "Hitler, According to Speer," in Canetti, *The*

Conscience of Words, trans. Joachim Neugroschel (New York: Seabury Press, 1979), 145–70. For Mao Tse-tung see the review by Jonathan Mirsky of the *Memoirs* of Mao's personal physician in *New York Review of Books* 19 (1994): 22–28. Mao's megalomania embraced the conviction that the death of even half the Chinese population in a nuclear war was no great loss.

[20] What Richir calls the frozen image of the one people, *Du sublime en politique,* 78. Cf. also Ferenc Feher's analysis of "proto-totalitarian political society," *The Frozen Revolution: An Essay on Jacobinism* (Cambridge: Cambridge UP, 1987).

[21] Arendt's theory of mass society is a simplification. The perception of radical atomization as the key to totalitarianism reveals a generational vision that Arendt shared with Horkheimer, Adorno and Canetti. The Weimar Republic was fragmented into groups rather than an atomized society. See Pierre Birnbaum, "Mass, Mobilization and the State" in C. Graumann and S. Moscovici, eds., *Changing Conceptions of Crowd Mind and Behaviour,* 177–201.

[22] The most powerful expression of war as the return to nature is Ernst Jünger's *In Stahlgewittern (Storms of Steel).* His later books *Total Mobilization* (1931) and *The Worker* (1932) apply the experience of total war to the totalitarian ideal of the selfless, robotic collective.

[23] See Thomas Mann's novella *Mario and the Magician* (1930), which is based on a close reading of Freud's *Group Psychology,* for a comparable exposition of the identity of the will and of obedience in the leader, the "Führer."

[24] *Georg Büchner: Complete Plays and Prose,* trans. Carl Richard Mueller (New York: Hill and Wang, 1963), 40–42. In the final sentence of the passage quoted, the translator omits the key word "sublime" (erhaben).

[25] Georg Büchner, *Complete Plays and Prose,* 41.

[26] Arendt, *The Human Condition* (Chicago: Chicago UP, 1958), 46–47.

[27] See "The Egalitarian State of Nature" and "The Egalitarian Millennium" in Norman Cohn, *The Pursuit of the Millennium* (London: Secker and Warburg, 1957).

[28] Urs Marti distinguishes between Canetti's negative vision of power, which he shares with Jakob Burckhardt and Michel Foucault, and Arendt's vision of the politically enabling dimensions of power, in his chapter, "Canettis Begriff der Macht im Lichte der Auffassungen von Hannah Arendt und Michel Foucault," in John Pattillo-Hess, ed., *Verwandlungsverbote und Befreiungsversuche in Canettis Masse und Macht* (Vienna: Löcker, 1991), 86–94.

Chapter 3

[1] A first approach is provided by John Pattillo-Hess, Mario R. Smole, eds., *Masse, Macht und Religion* (Vienna: Löcker, 1993).

[2] Axel Honneth, "The Perpetuation of the State of Nature: On the Cognitive Content of Elias Canetti's *Crowds and Power,*" in: *Thesis Eleven* 45(1996): 69–85.

[3] Ernst Cassirer: *The Myth of the State* (New Haven: Yale UP, 1946), 47.

[4] Max Weber: *The Sociology of Religion* (Boston: Beacon Press, 1993), 59.

[5] Elias Canetti, *Die Fackel im Ohr: Lebensgeschichte 1921–31* (Munich: Hanser, 1980), 140–41.

[6] Canetti, *Fackel im Ohr,* 160, 168.

[7] Ernst Fischer: *Erinnerungen und Reflexionen* (Reinbeck bei Hamburg: Rowohlt, 1969), 239.

[8] Canetti, *Fackel im Ohr,* 283.

[9] See Penka Angelova, "Das Konzept von Geschichte und Mythos bei Elias Canetti" in Penka Angelova, ed., *Die Massen und die Geschichte* (St. Ingbert, Germany: Röhrig, 1998), 55–87 and Herwig Gottwald, "Die Götter nach der Aufklärung: Zu Canettis Arbeit am Mythos" in the same work, 87–114.

[10] Emile Durkheim, *The Elementary Forms of the Religious Life* (London: Allen & Unwin, 1976), 209–10.

[11] Durkheim, *Elementary Forms,* 415.

[12] Honneth, "Perpetuation of the State of Nature," 78.

[13] See Ning Wu, *Canetti und China: Quellen, Materialien, Darstellung und Interpretation* (Stuttgart: Heinz, 2000).

[14] See Elsayed Elshahad's response to Canetti's interpretation of Islam, "Macht in Islam zwischen Theologie und Geschichte," in John Pattillo-Hess, ed., *Masse, Macht und Religion,* 127–35.

[15] Roberto Calasso, *Literature and the Gods* (London: Vintage, 2001), 173.

[16] Thomas Hobbes, *Leviathan* (Cambridge: Cambridge UP, 1991), 70. See Urs Marti, "Canettis *Masse und Macht* und die Genealogie der modernen politischen Philosophie," in Angelova, ed., *Die Masse in der Geschichte* 29–44.

[17] Cassirer, *Myth of the State,* 298.

[18] Christine Altvater and Petra Kuhnau both analyze the contradictions of what Canetti calls the moral squaring of the circle: Altvater, *"Die moralische Quadratur des Zirkels":* Zur Problematik der Macht in Elias Canettis Die Provinz des Menschen (Frankfurt: Lang, 1990); Kuhnau, *Masse und Macht in der Geschichte: Zur Konzeption anthropologischer Konstanten in Elias Canettis Werk Masse und Macht* (Würzburg: Königshausen & Neumann, 1996).

[19] See Urs Marti, "Canettis Masse und Macht," 42–43.

Chapter 4

[1] Cf. various writings of Anthony Giddens, Hans Joas, Michael Mann, and Alain Touraine, to mention only some of the most significant contributions to the debate. The work of Niklas Luhmann can arguably be seen as an attempt to deconstruct the dominant image from within.

[2] S. Moscovici, *The Age of the Crowd: A Historical Treatise on Mass Psychology* (Cambridge: Cambridge UP, 1985; originally published in French in 1981). For Moscovici's views on Canetti, cf. "Social Collectivities" in *Essays in Honour of Elias Canetti* (New York: Farrar, Straus & Giroux, 1987), 42–59, and "Ist die Idee der Masse noch aktuell?" in J. Pattillo-Hess, ed., *Canettis Masse und Macht oder die Aufgabe des gegenwärtigen Denkens* (Wien: Bundesverlag, 1988), 66–73. The latter text contains interesting reflections on the "invisible crowds" of the pacified postwar democracies.

[3] Canetti has consistently refused to engage with the sociological classics. The bibliography of *Crowds and Power* contains references to major anthropologists (e.g., Tylor, Boas, and Malinowski), but the founding fathers of sociology are conspicuously absent. (The closest thing to a sociological classic cited is Marcel Granet's work on China, but it seems to have been used as a sinological rather than a sociological text.)

[4] Moscovici, *The Age of the Crowd*, 1.

[5] Moscovici, *The Age of the Crowd*, 4–5.

[6] For a spirited demolition of Le Bon, see J. S. McClelland, *The Crowd and the Mob: From Plato to Canetti* (London: Unwin Hyman, 1989), 196–236.

[7] Moscovici, *The Age of the Crowd*, 77.

[8] For a more detailed critique of the sociological tradition from this point of view, cf. S. Moscovici, *La machine à faire des dieux* (Paris: Fayard, 1988).

[9] Sigmund Freud, "Massenpsychologie und Ich-Analyse," in *Gesammelte Werke*, vol. 13 (Frankfurt: Fischer, 1963), 74 (my translation, J. P. A). It has been pointed out that the use of the term "group psychology" in the English translation of this work obscures the connection with the older tradition of mass psychology. But it can also read as an oblique acknowledgment of Freud's interest in a general theory of social formations.

[10] Moscovici, *The Age of the Crowd*, 270.

[11] Moscovici, *The Age of the Crowd*, 271.

[12] Cf. Axel Honneth's paper, "The Perpetuation of the State of Nature: On the Cognitive Content of Elias Canetti's *Crowds and Power*," *Thesis Eleven* 45 (1996): 69–85; he ascribes to Canetti the claim that human conduct can be "explained in its entirety as the field of activity of bodily impulses which originate in the archaic nature of the human being." For an evolutionist interpretation, see R. Robertson, "Canetti als Anthropologe," in M. Krüger, ed., *Einladung zur Verwandlung: Essays zu Elias Canettis Masse und Macht* (Munich: Hanser, 1995), 190–206.

[13] Theodor Adorno, *Negative Dialectics* (London: Routledge & Kegan Paul, 1973), 355.

[14] For examples of such interpretations, see P. B. Armstrong, The *Phenomenology of Henry James* (New York: Columbia UP, 1983), and P. W. Silver, *Ortega as Phenomenologist* (New York: Columbia UP, 1978).

[15] For some reflections on this aspect of Canetti's thought, see E. Kiss, "Elias Canettis Phänomenologie der Masse oder eine Philosophie des Konkreten" in J. P. Strelka and Z. Szell, eds., *Ist Wahrheit ein Meer von Grashalmen? Zum Werk Elias Canettis* (Bern: Peter Lang, 1993), 111–20. However, this author uses an over-generalized notion of phenomenology (applicable even to post-structuralism), and this obscures the specific parallels noted above.

[16] At this point, a few words should be said about Canetti's terminology. The German title of *Crowds and Power* is *Masse und Macht*. Here the singular of the German word for "mass" is used, whereas both the critics of mass society and those who wanted to mobilize the masses for revolutionary purposes tended to prefer the plural. The reason for Canetti's choice seems obvious. He claimed to have defined the key characteristics of the phenomenon in question more adequately than other theorists; this was very much a matter of doing justice to its fundamental ambiguity and avoiding the symmetrical errors of admirers and detractors. But the ambiguity could only be fully understood as the obverse of a fundamental unity of crowd phenomena. McClelland's emphasis on the plural in the English title is therefore unfounded (he claims that Canetti wanted to underline the plurality of crowds, whereas mass psychology has found the singular more suitable; in fact, the original title of Le Bon's main work uses the plural: *foules*). But it is true that Canetti authorized the English title; he probably preferred the word "crowd" because of its less negative connotations (for a comparison of "crowd," "mob" and "masses," cf. McClelland, *The Crowd and the Mob*, 7–8).

[17] Elias Canetti. *Die gespaltene Zukunft* (Munich: Hanser, 1972), 120 (interview with J. Schickel, conducted in 1972; similar comments are made in the discussion with Adorno). In this context, Canetti also comments on what he thinks was Freud's most disastrous misconception: the postulate of the death drive, erroneously derived from the experience of the First World War. A thinker with particular pretensions to critical insight thus repeated in a more extreme form one of the cardinal sins of traditional thought: the naturalization of death.

[18] See Elias Canetti, *The Torch in my Ear* (New York: Farrar, Straus and Giroux, 1982), 118–24, 141–52. As this text shows, Canetti also saw Freud — or at least Freud's public image — as a model in a more fundamental sense: "People talked about him in such a way as if every individual could, by himself, of his own accord and at his own resolve, find explanations for things" (122). This vision of single-handed defiance of the intellectual division of labor remained intact, despite his growing disagreement with Freud's theories. Some indications of the projected alternative to psychoanalysis can be gleaned from the discussion with Adorno. In particular, Canetti singles out the concept of identification, which he thinks does more to obscure than to explain the transforming processes involved in relationships to role-models. We can assume that a fully developed theory of transformation would — among other things — have generated an alternative account of psychic development.

[19] E. Durkheim, *The Elementary Forms of the Religious Life* (London: Allen & Unwin, 1976), 218.

[20] Canetti's extreme aversion to the Romans (whom he describes as having "absolute dignity, but no humanity") is a logical consequence of his more general attitude to power. Rome "conquered Christianity by becoming Christendom" (*PM*, 44) and subsequently became a permanent model of conquest and plundering. Canetti fears that "the earth may be destroyed by the heritage of the Romans" (*PM*, 44). But it is worth noting that at the same time (1943), he was reflecting on the course of the Second World War and suggesting that the powers most indebted to Roman models (the Germans and the Japanese) were for that reason fatally disadvantaged (*PM*, 62–63).

[21] Elias Canetti, *The Play of the Eyes* (New York: Farrar, Straus and Giroux, 1986), 89.

[22] Both "transformation" and "metamorphosis" have been used to translate Canetti's *Verwandlung*; in line with the English version of *Crowds and Power* I have used the former, but it should be noted that it may lead to misunderstandings: Canetti's concept goes far beyond the transformative capacity that is thematized in some theories of social action and social change.

[23] McClelland (*The Crowd and the Mob*) rightly emphasizes Canetti's break with traditional views on the relationship between crowds and power, but the contrast between "the sanity of crowds and the madness of power" (*CP*, 293) is overdrawn. The crowd phenomenon as analyzed by Canetti is far too ambiguous and multifaceted to justify such a dichotomy. It would seem more appropriate to say that Canetti saw complex and often conflictual interaction where earlier theorists had mostly seen unilateral dependence. In this connection, Canetti's comments on Machiavelli are of some interest. As he saw it, the latter "studied power in the same way as I study crowds" (*NH*, 11). We should probably read this as a double-edged statement. On the one hand, Canetti admits that there is a lesson to be learned from Machiavelli: the open-minded and dispassionate analysis of power is still a model for the study of crowds. On the other hand, Machiavelli's objectivity and intellectual flexibility were ultimately misapplied: he failed to grasp power as the absolute evil that it is (and that the crowd is not).

[24] In the interview with Schickel (see note 17), Canetti contrasts his own use of myths with Lévi-Strauss's structuralist version of comparative mythology. He accepts the general principle that primitive and civilized societies should be compared on equal terms, but objects to the comparative shortcut which abstracts from the content of myths in order to highlight the underlying common themes. As he sees it, philosophical anthropology is the proper framework for a comparative study of societies and civilizations; if myths are to be put to productive use in this context, we must respect the narrative singularity that is their hallmark and resist the temptation to collapse them into the comparative project which should be capable of learning from them without denaturing them. Further critical remarks on Lévi-Strauss are to be

found in the last collection of aphorisms (*Aufzeichnungen 1992–1993*, [Munich: Hanser, 1996], 68–69): "How can a man who has swallowed thousands of myths fail to understand that they are the very opposite of a system?" Canetti then speculates about the reasons for Lévi-Strauss's fundamental misunderstanding and mentions several of them, including an "absolute need for order," an obsession with institutions and an uncritical transfer of methods and categories from the study of kinship to the study of myths.

Chapter 5

[1] Hannah Arendt, *The Origins of Totalitarianism*, 3rd ed. (London: Allen and Unwin, 1967).

[2] Leo Strauss, *The Political Philosophy of Hobbes: Its Basis and its Genesis* (Chicago: Chicago UP, 1952), viii.

[3] Leo Strauss, *The Political Philosophy of Hobbes*, 5.

[4] Franz Borkenau, *Der Übergang vom feudalen zum bürgerlichen Weltbild: Studien zur Geschichte der Philosophie der Manufakturperiode* (Darmstadt: Wissenschaftliche Buchgesellschaft, 1976), 467.

[5] Franz Borkenau, *Der Übergang vom feudalen zum bürgerlichen Weltbild*, 482.

[6] Franz Borkenau, *Der Übergang vom feudalen zum bürgerlichen Weltbild*, 466.

[7] Thomas Hobbes, *Leviathan* (Cambridge: Cambridge UP, 1991), 62.

[8] Thomas Hobbes, *Leviathan*, 70. See also the discussion of Hobbes in chapter 3.

[9] Cornelius Castoriadis, "Anthropology, Philosophy, Politics," *Thesis Eleven* 49 (1997): 103.

[10] See Jan Assmann, *Herrschaft und Heil* (München: Beck, 2000).

[11] See Jean-Pierre Vernant, *Les origines de la pensée grecque* (Paris: Presses Universitaires de la France, 1992).

[12] See Jean-Pierre Vernant et al., *Divination et rationalité* (Paris: Seuil, 1978).

[13] Léon Vandermeersch, "L'imaginaire divinatoire dans l'histoire de la Chine," *Bulletin de l'Ecole Française de l'Extrème-Orient* 79:1 (1992): 1–8. An ingenious modern Japanese variation on the Taoist theme of sagehood inaccessible to power is to be found in Mori Ogai's short story, "Kazan Jittoku," in David Dilworth and J. Thomas Rimer, eds., *The Incident at Sakai and Other Stories*, vol. 1 of *The Historical Stories of Mori Ogai* (Honolulu: Hawaii UP, 1977), 205–14.

[14] See especially Patricia Crone, *Meccan Trade and the Rise of Islam* (Princeton: Princeton UP, 1987).

[15] For the most sustained argument of this kind, see Roger Boesche, *Theories of Tyranny: From Plato to Arendt* (University Park, PA: U of Pennsylvania P, 1996).

Works Cited

Adorno, Theodor. *Negative Dialectics.* London: Routledge and Kegan Paul, 1973.

Altvater, Christine. *"Die moralische Quadratur des Zirkels": Zur Problematik der Macht in Elias Canettis Die Provinz des Menschen.* Frankfurt: Lang, 1990.

Angelova, Penka, "Das Konzept von Geschichte und Mythos bei Elias Canetti." In Angelova, ed. *Die Massen und die Geschichte.* St. Ingbert, Germany: Röhrig, 1998, 55–87.

———, ed. *Die Massen und die Geschichte.* St. Ingbert, Germany: Röhrig, 1998.

Arendt, Hannah. *The Human Condition.* Chicago: Chicago UP, 1958.

———. *The Origins of Totalitarianism.* 3rd ed. London: Allen and Unwin, 1967.

Armstrong, P. B. *The Phenomenology of Henry James.* New York: Columbia UP, 1983.

Arnason, Johann P. "The Dialectic of Enlightenment and the Post-Functionalist Theory of Society," in *Thesis Eleven* 13 (1986): 77–93.

Assmann, Jan. *Herrschaft und Heil.* Munich: Beck, 2000.

Bellow, Saul. *Herzog.* Harmondsworth, England: Penguin, 1965.

Benjamin, Walter. *The Origin of German Tragic Drama.* Translated by John Osborne. London: NLB, 1977.

Blumenberg, Hans. "Ernst Cassirers gedenkend." In Blumenberg, *Wirklichkeiten in denen wir leben.* Stuttgart: Reclam, 1981.

Boesche, Roger. *Theories of Tyranny: From Plato to Arendt.* University Park: U of Pennsylvania P, 1996.

Borkenau, Franz. *Der Übergang vom feudalen zum bürgerlichen Weltbild: Studien zur Geschichte der Philosophie der Manufakturperiode.* Darmstadt: Wissenschaftliche Buchgesellschaft, 1976 (originally published 1934).

Büchner, Georg. *Complete Plays and Prose.* Translated by Carl Richard Mueller. New York: Hill and Wang, 1963.

Calasso, Roberto. *Literature and the Gods.* London: Vintage, 2001.

Canetti, Elias. *Aufzeichnungen 1992–1993.* Munich: Hanser, 1996.

———. *Auto da Fé*. Translated by C. V. Wedgwood. Harmondsworth, England: Penguin, 1973.

———. *Crowds and Power*. Translated by Carol Stewart. Harmondsworth, England: Penguin, 1973.

———. "Das erste Buch." In Herbert Göpfert, ed. *Canetti lesen*. Munich: Hanser, 1975.

———. *Die Fackel im Ohr: Lebensgeschichte 1921–31*. Munich: Hanser, 1980.

———. *Das Geheimherz der Uhr: Aufzeichnungen 1973–1985*. Munich: Hanser, 1987.

———. *Die gespaltene Zukunft*. Munich: Hanser, 1972.

———. "Hitler, According to Speer." In Canetti. *The Conscience of Words*. Translated by Joachim Neugroschel. New York: Seabury Press, 1979.

———. *Nachträge aus Hampstead. Aus den Aufzeichnungen 1954–1971*. Munich: Hanser, 1994.

———. *The Play of the Eyes*. New York: Farrar, Straus and Giroux, 1986.

———. *Die Provinz des Menschen. Aufzeichnungen 1942–1972*. Munich: Hanser, 1973.

———. *The Torch in My Ear*. New York: Farrar, Straus and Giroux, 1986.

Cardonnoy, Eric Leroy du. *Les Réflexions d'Elias Canetti: une esthétique de la discontinuité*. Bern: Lang, 1997.

Cassirer, Ernst. *The Myth of the State*. New Haven, CT: Yale UP, 1946.

———. *The Philosophy of Symbolic Forms*, Vol. I: *Language*. Translated by Ralph Manheim. Vol II: *Mythical Thought*. Translated by Ralph Manheim. New Haven, CT: Yale UP, 1955.

Castoriadis, Cornelius. "Anthropology, Philosophy, Politics." *Thesis Eleven* 49 (1997): 99–116.

———. *The Imaginary Institution of Society*. Translated by Kathleen Blamey. Cambridge: Polity Press, 1987.

Cohn, Norman. *The Pursuit of the Millennium*. London: Secker and Warburg, 1957.

Crone, Patricia. *Meccan Trade and the Rise of Islam*. Princeton, NJ: Princeton UP, 1987.

Donahue, William Collins. *End of Modernism: Elias Canetti's Auto-da-Fe*. Chapel Hill: U of North Carolina P, 2001.

Durkheim, Emile. *The Elementary Forms of the Religious Life*. London: Allen & Unwin, 1976.

Elbaz, Robert, and Leah Hadomi. *Elias Canetti or the Failing of the Novel*. New York: Lang, 1995.

Elias, Norbert. *The Civilizing Process: Sociogenetic and Psychogenetic Investigations*. Oxford: Blackwell, 2000.

———. *The Society of Individuals*. Edited by Michael Schröter and translated by Edmund Jephcott. Oxford: Blackwell, 1991.

———. *Über den Prozess der Zivilisation: Soziogenetische und psychogenetische Untersuchungen*. Vol. 1. Frankfurt: Suhrkamp, 1977.

Elshahad, Elsayed. "Macht in Islam zwischen Theologie und Geschichte." In John Pattillo-Hess, ed., *Masse, Macht und Religion*. Vienna: Löcker, 1993, 127–35.

Engelmann, Susanne. *Babel — Bibel — Bibliothek: Canettis Aphorismen zur Sprache*. Würzburg: Könighausen and Neumann, 1997.

Essays in Honour of Elias Canetti. New York: Farrar, Straus & Giroux, 1987.

Feher, Ferenc. *The Frozen Revolution: An Essay on Jacobinism*. Cambridge: Cambridge UP, 1987.

Fetscher, Iring. "*Masse und Macht* und die Erklärung totalitärer Gesellschaften." In John Pattillo-Hess, ed. *Verwandlungsverbote und Befreiungsversuche in Canettis Masse und Macht*. Vienna, Löcker, 1991.

Fischer, Ernst. *Erinnerungen und Reflexionen*. Reinbeck bei Hamburg: Rowohlt, 1969.

Freud, Sigmund. "Civilization and its Discontents." In *The Penguin Freud Library XII*. London: Penguin, 1991.

———. "The Future of an Illusion." in *The Penguin Freud Library XII*. London: Penguin, 1991.

———. *Gesammelte Werke*. Vol. 14. Frankfurt: Fischer, 1963.

———. "Group Psychology and the Analysis of the Ego." In *The Penguin Freud Library* XII. London, Penguin, 1991.

Gauchet, Marcel. *The Disenchantment of the World: A Political History of Religion*. Translated by Oscar Burge. Princeton, NJ: Princeton UP, 1997.

Godé, Maurice, Ingrid Haag, and Jacques Le Rider, eds. "Wien-Berlin: Deux sites de la modernité." *Cahiers d'Études Germaniques* 24 (1993).

Gottwald, Herwig, "Die Götter nach der Aufklärung: Zu Canettis Arbeit am Mythos." In *Die Massen und die Geschichte*. St. Ingbert, Germany: Röhrig, 1998.

Hennighaus, Lothar. *Tod und Verwandlung: Elias Canettis poetische Anthropologie aus der Kritik der Psychoanalyse.* Frankfurt: Lang, 1984.

Hesse, Hermann. *Steppenwolf.* Translated by Basil Creighton. New York: Holt, Rinehart and Winston, n.d.

Hobbes, Thomas. *Leviathan.* Cambridge: Cambridge UP, 1991.

Honneth, Axel. "The Perpetuation of the State of Nature: On the Cognitive Content of Elias Canetti's *Crowds and Power.*" *Thesis Eleven* 45 (1996): 69–85.

Horkheimer, Max, and Theodor W. Adorno. *Dialectic of Enlightenment.* Translated by John Cumming. London: Allen Lane, 1973.

Jünger, Ernst. *Der Arbeiter.* Stuttgart: Klett, 1981.

Kiss, Endre. "Elias Canetti's Phänomenologie der Masse oder eine Philosophie des Konkreten." In Joseph P. Strelka and Zsuzsa Szell, eds.. *Ist Wahrheit ein Meer von Grashalmen? Zum Werk Elias Canettis.* Bern: Peter Lang, 1993, 111–20.

Klages, Ludwig. *Der Geist als Widersacher der Seele.* 3 vols. Leipzig: Barth, 1929–1933.

Koch, Werner, ed. *Selbstanzeige: Schriftsteller im Gespräch.* Frankfurt: Fischer, 1971.

König, Helmut. *Zivilisation und Leidenschaften. Die Masse im bürgerlichen Zeitalter.* Reinbek bei Hamburg: Rowohlt, 1992.

Krüger, Michael, ed. *Einladung zur Verwandlung: Essays zu Elias Canettis Masse und Macht.* Munich: Hanser, 1995.

Kuhnau, Petra. *Masse und Macht in der Geschichte: Zur Konzeption anthropologischer Konstanten in Elias Canettis Werk Masse und Macht.* Würzburg: Königshausen & Neumann, 1996.

Le Rider, Jacques. *Modernity and Crises of Identity: Culture and Society in Fin-de-Siecle Vienna.* Translated by Rosemary Morris. Cambridge: Polity Press, 1993.

Lukács, Georg. *History and Class Consciousness: Studies in Marxist Dialectics.* Translated by Rodney Livingstone. London: Merlin Press, 1971.

Mack, Michael. *Anthropology as Memory: Elias Canetti's and Franz Baermann Steiner's Responses to the Shoah.* Tübingen: Niemayer, 2001.

Marti, Urs. "Canettis Begriff der Macht im Lichte der Auffassungen von Hannah Arendt und Michel Foucault." In John Pattillo-Hess, ed. *Verwandlungsverbote und Befreiungsversuche in Canettis Masse und Macht.* Vienna: Löcker, 1991.

———. "Canetti's *Masse und Macht* und die Genealogie der modernen politischen Philosophie." In Penke Angelovna, ed. *Die Masse in der Geschichte.* St. Ingbert, Germany: Röhrig, 1998.

Matt, Peter von. "Der phantastische Aphorismus bei Elias Canetti." In Adrian Stevens and Fred Wagner, eds. *Elias Canetti: Londoner Symposium.* Stuttgart: Heinz, 1991.

McClelland, J. S. *The Crowd and the Mob from Plato to Canetti.* London: Unwin Hyman, 1989.

Mori, Ogai. "Kazan Jittoku." In David Dilworth and J. Thomas Rimer, eds. *The Incident at Sakai and Other Stories: Vol. 1 of the Historical Stories of Mori Ogai.* Honolulu: Hawaii UP, 1977.

Moscovici, Serge. *The Age of the Crowd.* Cambridge: Cambridge UP, 1985.

———. "The Discovery of the Masses" in Carol Graumann and S. Moscovici, eds. *Changing Conceptions of Crowd Mind and Behaviour.* New York/Berlin: Springer, 1986.

———. *La machine à faire des dieux.* Paris: Fayard, 1988.

———. "Social Collectivities." In *Essays in Honour of Elias Canetti.* Translated by Michael Hulse. London: Andre Deutsch, 1987.

Neumann, Gerhard. "Widerrufe des Sündenfalls." In *Hüter der Verwandlung.* Munich: Hanser, 1985.

Pattillo-Hess, John, ed. *Canettis Masse und Macht oder die Aufgabe des gegenwärtigen Denkens.* Wien: Bundesverlag, 1988.

———, ed. *Verwandlungsverbote und Befreiungsversuche in Canettis Masse und Macht.* Vienna: Löcker, 1991.

Pattillo-Hess, John, and Mario R. Smole, eds. *Canettis Aufstand gegen Macht und Tod.* Vienna: Löcker, 1996.

———, eds. *Masse, Macht und Religion.* Vienna: Löcker, 1993.

Pöder, Elfriede. "Spurensicherung: Otto Weininger in der Blendung." In Friedrich Aspetsberger and Gerard Stieg, eds. *Blendung als Lebensform: Elias Canetti.* Königstein: Athenäum, 1985.

Richir, Marc. *Du sublime en politique.* Paris: Payot, 1991.

Riedner, Nicola. *Canettis Fischerle: Eine Figur zwischen Masse, Macht und Blendung.* Würzburg: Königshausen & Neumann, 1994.

Roberts, David. "Die Blendung der gesamten Romanliteratur: Bemerkungen zu Canettis paradoxer Romanpoetik." In Gerhard Neumann, ed. *Canetti als Leser.* Freiburg: Rombach, 1996.

———. *Kopf und Welt: Canettis Roman Die Blendung.* Munich: Hanser, 1975.

———. "The Sense of an Ending: Apocalyptic Perspectives in the 20th century German Novel." *Orbis Litterarum* 32 (1977): 140–58.

Rohrwasser, Michael. "Elias Canettis Auseinandersetzung mit der Psychoanalyse in seinem Roman Die Blendung." *Convivium* (2000): 43–64.

Schmid-Bortenschlager, Sigrid. "Der Einzelne und seine Masse: Massentheorie und Literaturkonzeption bei Elias Canetti und Hermann Broch." In Kurt Bartsch and Gerhard Melzer, eds. *Experte der Macht: Elias Canetti*. Graz: Droschl, 1985.

Schnädelbach, Herbert. *Philosophie in Deutschland 1831–1933*. Frankfurt: Suhrkamp, 1994.

Schorske, Carl. "Politics in a New Key." In *Fin-de-Siècle Vienna: Politics and Culture*. New York: Knopf, 1980.

Silver, P. W. *Ortega as Phenomenologist*. New York: Columbia UP, 1978.

Simmel, Georg. *The Conflict of Form and Other Essays*. Translated by K. Peter Etzkorn. New York: Teachers College Press, 1968.

———. "The Tragedy of Culture." In David Frisby and Mike Featherstone, eds. *Simmel on Culture: Selected Writings*. London: Sage, 1997.

Sorel, Georges. *Reflections on Violence*. New York: Collier Books, 1961.

Söring, Jürgen. "Die Literatur als Provinz des Menschen." *Deutsche Vierteljahrsschrift für Literaturwissenschaft* 60 (1986).

Sternhall, Zeev, with Mario Sznejder and Maria Ashari. *The Birth of Fascist Ideology: From Cultural Rebellion to Political Revolt*. Translated by David Maisel. Princeton, NJ: Princeton UP, 1994.

Stieg, Gerard. "Canetti und die Psychoanalyse: Das Unbehagen in der Kultur und Die Blendung." In Adrian Stevens and Fred Wagner, eds. *Elias Canetti. Londoner Symposium*. Stuttgart: Heinz, 1991.

Strauss, Leo. *The Political Philosophy of Hobbes: Its Basis and its Genesis*. Chicago: U of Chicago P, 1952.

Vandermeersch, Léon. "L'imaginaire divinatoire dans l'histoire de la Chine." *Bulletin de L 'École Française de l'Extrême-Orient* 79:1 (1992), 1–8.

Vernant, Jean-Pierre. *Les origines de la pensée grecque*. Paris: Presses Universitaires de France, 1992.

Vernant, Jean-Pierre et al. *Divination et rationalité*. Paris: Editions du Seuil, 1978.

Weber, Max. *The Sociology of Religion*. Boston: Beacon Press, 1993.

Weigel, Robert. "Elias Canettis Masse und Macht und Hermann Brochs Massenwahntheorie: Berührungspunkte und Unterschiede." In Joseph P. Strelka and Zsuzsa Szell, eds. *Ist die Wahrheit ein Meer vom Grashalmen? In Zum Werk Elias Canettis*. Bern: Lang, 1993.

Wu, Ning. *Canetti und China: Quellen, Materialien, Darstellung und Interpretation*. Stuttgart: Heinz, 2000.

Zepp, Peter. *Privatmythos und Wahn: Das mythopoetische Konzept im Werk Elias Canettis*. Frankfurt: Lang, 1990.

Zopotoczky, N. S. "Canettis Massentheorie zwischen Adler und Broch." In John Pattillo-Hess, ed. *Canettis Masse und Macht oder Die Aufgabe des gegenwärtigen Denkens*. Vienna: Bundesverlag, 1988.

Index